ANTIQUES

A Guide to Sensible Buying

ANTIQUES

A Guide to Sensible Buying

PATRICK McVEIGH

JOHN DONALD PUBLISHERS LTD
EDINBURGH

To
Una

© John Donald Publishers Ltd., 1974

ISBN 0 85976 003 0

Printed in Great Britain
by Alden & Mowbray Ltd
at the Alden Press, Oxford

Preface

In the last few years, antiques have become one of the major growth industries. Shops open in the most unlikely of places and often with the most unlikely stock. Signs blossom above doorways proclaiming, some factually and some hopefully, the magic word *Antiques*. Authorities and authors, lecturers and specialists proliferate, and as always, in a boom situation with a credulous buying public, the speculators, the market manipulators and the plain con men have moved in on the act.

This is yet another book on antiques. It is not however a specialist's book, for as a dealer depending largely on trade business, I cannot afford the luxury of stocking only my own particular preferences. Although the range of subjects discussed in this book is a fairly varied one, what is commonly referred to as *Victoriana* has no place in it. The products of the Victorian period, that is of the 19th century from about the year 1840 onwards, were in the main the result of an industrialised society with the productive forces based on mechanical power, a situation quite distinct and until then unique in human experience. This period is not to be denigrated or sneered at, yet in my view it is beyond the scope of the genuine antique dealer or collector for the reasons I have given.

Similarly ignored are the various art cults and 'movements' of the present century, some no doubt very worthy of attention but not—let us get our definitions right—as antiques.

Still less is this book claimed as being of value to the investor. That is not to say that the things I have bought and will continue to buy have not gone up in price. I cannot think of anything I have sold that I would not gladly buy back today, giving the seller at least a reasonable profit over his original price and allowing also for the effects of inflation.

There is a widespread idea, largely cultivated by collectors and dealers with particular financial interests, that all antiques have increased in value and will continue to do so but this is in fact very far from the truth. An interesting exercise can be undertaken by any sensible person simply by consulting old copies of such a magazine as *The Connoisseur*. There he will find that many classes of antiques, such as Chinese export porcelain and miniature paintings, fetched more in real money terms sixty years ago than they do today. Some things indeed, such as engravings, which reached very large sums then, are in many cases virtually unsaleable now, while to take another instance, oak furniture of the seventeenth century is only now appreciating in value to the level it held in the period before the First World War.

This then is definitely not a book for the person who is interested in buying antiques purely as an investment. Such things as Pot Lids, Fairings, Silk Pictures and the weird, inflated and often manipulated prices they obtain, are not my concern.

The kind of person who I believe will find this book of real value is the person who has a love of antiques and a modest income which shows an occasional surplus of a few pounds. Whether it be building a specialized collection, or buying for the sheer love of something, or often, for the more immediate purpose of house furnishing, I believe it is still possible and in Britain at least, *always will be possible*, to buy quality antiques at prices comparable with the same sort of article purchased new. To do this, one must be ready to disregard conventional attitudes and fashionable pressures and try to look at things afresh, with enthusiasm, knowledge and, above all, with love.

With few exceptions, the illustrations in this book are of articles which have at one time or another been purchased by me from various antique shops in Scotland and the North of England. Illustrations taken from museums and famous collections may be very lovely, but in my view they have limited relevance to the ordinary buyer and collector.

The photographs were taken by members of *The Scotsman* staff and I am indebted to that newspaper for permission to reproduce these and also to reprint the material for this book which is largely based upon articles originally published in *The Scotsman*.

My thanks also to Mr Willis Pickard for his help and encouragement.

Patrick McVeigh   Edinburgh, 1974

Prices
Bearing in mind the fluctuations in rates of exchange, the North American reader may find it helpful to multiply by approximately two and a half the Sterling figures given, in order to arrive at the dollar equivalent.

Contents

1   Some Guidelines to Buying

I would like to begin by making both an emphatic statement and a definition. Contrary to general opinion both inside the antique trade and on the part of the public as a whole, many antiques, far from being too dear, are still ludicrously under-priced, and in fact, to use a much debased word in its original and honest sense, they are too cheap. By antiques I mean articles of age, craftsmanship, quality and provenance, usually attractive and often beautiful: very often both useful and functional under present day conditions of life.

I have given the above definition at some length because I intend largely to ignore the Victorian and later eras, not because I am pedantic enough to believe that craftsmanship and beauty stopped short at some arbitary dateline, but rather for the reason that time does indeed winnow fine and, as I wish to show, one of the main pitfalls in antique buying is to follow a fashionable trend which is, alas, usually transient both in terms of taste and in monetary value.

As a practical antique dealer of the type who is very much a 'loner'—that is, who does not buy at auctions or is not part of a 'ring' or shipping consortium (not, I hasten to add, because I have anything against these methods of dealing except that I find them tedious and boring) I have evolved a rough but reliable index of value both current and future.

This, like a carefully chosen stockbroker's portfolio, has given me not merely a good living but also on the whole a worthwhile and appreciating investment in both shop stock and personal possessions. Although one may disapprove of the idea as a private individual of buying antiques primarily as an investment, one must as a dealer who wishes to stay in business, consider very carefully both purchasing and future selling prices.

Basic Rules

My own guide to buying, then, is basically this. I first ask myself when looking at an item: 'Do I like it?', and if so, is the price such that it would be either impossible to reproduce or the cost of making a reasonably satisfactory reproduction be much higher than the cost of the genuine article? On the basis of the application of this rule, one can readily see that the present prices of many, many antiques are not merely low but they have yet a long way to travel before they reach their ceiling, and conversely (this is where I will tread on a few toes), a

1

great number of antiques are sadly over-priced and have, to my eye at least, a decidedly uncertain future.

I propose now to examine a few examples of both the former and latter categories.

First of all, one could fitly commence with the subject of silver. Until about the spring of 1969, there was a great deal of money floating about this country with nothing particular to do and silver prices took an enormous boom largely as a result of speculative investment. For a while it seemed that anything with a hallmark would sell. Indeed, some of the hallmarks I saw on articles with three-figure prices on them, were so rubbed as to be largely a combination of optimism and imagination. No matter, they sold, together with Georgian silver re-hammered in the Victorian manner, the most atrociously ugly Victorian tea services, and anything which had been patched, beaten or hammered into some kind of shape.

Today people are saying, 'The bottom has dropped out of the silver market.' 'Don't touch it with a bargepole,' etc., but in my view nothing could be farther from the truth, and the truth is that good quality silver will always be a sound long-term investment and a source of delight to the eye. In the form of flatware, it is the best and in the long run the cheapest method of conveying food from the plate to the mouth.

At present one can buy good quality late-eighteenth- and early-nineteenth-century silver tableware at £4 to £5 per ounce. Compare this with modern tableware, both in silver and in plate, and it will be readily seen that in the long run, buying good, sound, wellmarked, Georgian silver flatware is one of the most practical things to do with any spare cash you have.

With discretion and a longer purse, the same rules apply to most Georgian household silver, especially if one takes the trouble to buy Continental pieces, which are often of high quality but equally often, in Britain at least, at moderate prices. The fashionable collectors' items like vinaigrettes are decidedly to be avoided as prices here have risen to ludicrous heights and are to my mind now grossly over-priced. Compare, for instance, a Georgian vinaigrette at £50 or so with a needlecase of the same period at about £10 and you will see what I mean.

Longcase or 'Grandfather' Clocks

Despite talk of a slump in the antique trade, prices continue upwards but none more steadily than that of Longcase or 'Grandfather' clocks.

Typical 'Grandfather' or Longcase clock. Scottish c. 1780.

Mention, as recently as three years ago, a painted face longcase clock to a dealer in the toffee-nosed end of the trade and all you got in reply would be a faint sniff, turning to a positive sneer if you had the temerity to add that your clock had an oak case.

Today, dealers are scouring the country only too willing to pay £70 to £120 for painted face clocks of the late eighteenth and early nineteenth centuries, and even those cheery Victorian country horrors with every conceivable ornament on face and case are snapped up. A couple of years ago I put all the money I obtained from the sale of a valuable manuscript into the purchase of 'cheap' longcase clocks. I have sold them all long since and I would willingly buy them back, giving the purchasers a profit on each one.

The reason, of course, is not hard to find. One can still find for £90 to £150 a top quality eight-day movement clock with a handsome inlaid case, often with a dial painted in the most charming fashion. A clock of country oak of the same period should cost £80 to £90 if in perfect working order, and although the case may lack inlay it will be elegant in its own simple way.

Prices rise continually and it is easily seen why. These clocks were made in enormous numbers but they have been shipped out of the country by the thousand and are rapidly becoming so scarce that they will be difficult to buy at all before their price rises to the full value which I estimate as between two and three times their present level. Just look at the workmanship of the clockmaker and cabinetmaker and you will see what I mean, and remember that the movement of most eight-day painted face clocks of the late eighteenth century is just about the same quality as that of their brass-faced counterparts. You are, in other words, paying £100 to £150 more for a brass face, and indeed, I know a clever little chap who works wonders in brass . . . but that is another story!

Porcelain

On the whole, European porcelain of quality is now so expensive that even the high quality fakes obligingly manufactured by Samson of Paris are overpriced. On the other hand, Britain was the first country in the world to make earthenware with a white body and a translucent glaze and this was of a quality since unsurpassed by any other ceramic techniques. There is still a great deal of this early ware around in all shapes and sorts and much of it remains at very modest prices, although it is naturally becoming scarcer and rising steadily in value.

Take a common or garden piece of English Underglaze Blue on White in your hand and the potting is so light and precise, so 'tight' that it actually sings in your fingers. There will be either a beautifully

4

made foot ring or no foot ring at all. It may be marked 'Spode', 'Riley', 'Rogers' or unmarked, it is little or no matter. Look at the beautiful depth of blue, the precision of the transfer printing, the authenticity of the botanical border, and most of all the charm and absolute veracity of English country scenes it depicts.

All this grace and beauty for any home can still be purchased for a price ranging from two pounds to (except in the case of very rare specimens) under fifteen pounds for large serving plates of the highest standard of earthen potting that was ever made. Indeed the surprising thing about English Blue on White is that it is now becoming fairly scarce without its price having risen to a very great degree.

As for other eighteenth-century white earthenware, I can only point out the contrast, that while ridiculous sums are being paid for late Victorian 'flatback' figures (Dick Turpin, Garibaldi and so on), the best of English and Scottish ware of almost a century earlier can still be purchased for substantially less. Figures of delicacy, charm and vitality can be obtained for around £40 to £80 each and mugs and jugs, teapots, and tepoys often much lower.

Imperfect Pieces

I refer here to some prices for perfect specimens, but really rare and beautiful ware from such centres as Leeds, Prestonpans, Bristol and Liverpool can still be purchased in slightly imperfect condition at prices ranging from £10 to £30. I know, of course, that most books on ceramics advise one to buy only perfect specimens but in my opinion. the writers of these books are now out of touch with reality, for perfect specimens of any early wares are now rare and, while it is always best to buy items in perfect condition, it can be both dear and risky.

Good quality restoration is much more common than the odd piece which has survived in mint condition. It always amuses me to see a dealer eagerly snap up an article of damaged Delft ware and at the same time pass up earthenware made in the same period but slightly damaged, though often much rarer and more desirable.

Never forget, dealers can be and often are creatures of habit, just as we all tend to be. They are used to palmier days when Delft for instance had to be in polychrome before it was considered worth buying, when English soft paste in underglaze blue was worth only a few shillings and then only for jugs and sauceboats.

Every day, I buy damaged wares and I have done so for years. Early lustre ware, resist lustre, commemorative jugs (last month a beautiful and important early Wedgwood creamware jug depicting the death of Wolfe on the Plains of Abraham for £5), Sunderland, Liverpool, Portobello, Musselburgh, there is not a single piece of this type that I have sold, even recently, that I would not buy back again and gladly allow a profit to the original purchasers.

I hope now that I have set my theme in motion, potential buyers may think for themselves of the widely varied opportunities before them, for Britain, despite years of shipping antiques abroad, has still an amazing richness of collectable antiques, far more than any other country in the world. The important thing is to try and work by the rules I have outlined and to the lasting pleasures your purchases will give, a continuing bonus in appreciation in value will be added.

2 The Fakers

The upsurge of interest in antiques, so notable in the last few years, coupled with the ever-diminishing amount of quality articles on the market, has presented a golden opportunity for the unscrupulous dealer to line his pockets at the expense of an often all too gullible public.

Most people, when thinking of antique fakers, have visions of some forged 'masterpiece' in painting or a carefully 'restored' article of quality furniture. The real market, however, and the real money, lies in the more modest end of the trade, where many thousands of people spend sums of from five to fifty pounds.

This is the mass market for the antique faker. The fairly modest sums involved in each transaction make it comparatively easy for the unscrupulous, or often, as is now the case, the downright ignorant dealer, to pass off a piece as genuine to a purchaser who has little knowledge and is forced to rely on the assurances given to him by the dealer.

Despite the Trade Descriptions Act, which was framed to protect consumers from the consequences of false and misleading descriptions of goods (including antiques), the faking goes on, and indeed increases as the trade itself grows and operates in a situation of increasing scarcity.

Glass

Let us take a look at some of the most common forms of faking, examples of which can be seen today in literally dozens of 'antique' shops in Britain.

The market for 'cut' and 'cased' glass is a very large and often not too discriminating one. 'Cased' glass is the trade description of nineteenth-century glass which has a coloured overlay on top of a clear layer of glass. This top layer is then partially cut away in various designs, producing a very attractive effect.

Today, however, very large amounts of what appears at first glance to be this type of glass is being produced in the Chinese Peoples' Republic and is widely sold as the genuine article. These copies can be produced at a fraction of the cost of the real thing since the colour is merely painted on and made fast by re-heating the glass, while the cut effect is achieved by casting the glass in moulds in the required pattern.

One old-established family antique business known to me, are now regarded almost as specialists in this particular line, and they sell not merely to the public but also to the trade.

Weapons

The interest in Militaria, represented mainly by edged weapons and guns, has grown enormously in recent years and, as always, the sharp merchant has moved in to help fill the demand.

Good copies of pistols and long guns, especially the easier to copy percussion actions, are made in North Africa and are coming on to the British market in large quantities. Recently, these copies have been fetching about £30 each in Scottish salerooms, while they can be purchased 'wholesale' in Italy for about £8 each.

The traditional Scottish Highland sword, which is usually though incorrectly called a Claymore but is accurately described as a Basket Hilt Broadsword, always has a ready market, and good early examples fetch over three figures, while Victorian and modern (i.e., Army) specimens sell readily, unfortunately often passed off as much earlier than their true period. Much worse than this is the practice of 'marrying up' geniune baskets, large numbers of which have survived, to reproduction or old but incorrect blades.

Pewter and Copper

Pewter and copper articles have an almost universal appeal, and the type of faking carried out here is on real factory lines. Several very respectable antique trade journals carry regular advertisements for these manufacturers, such as the firm who advertise their pewter as bearing genuine William and Mary 'touch' marks. The copper articles, although not cheap, are often quite well made and supply the enormous tourist demand for things like coaching horns, carriage lamps and warming pans.

With pewter, however, the faker can really go to town, for pewter prices have soared recently, out of all proportion to true value, and, as always, a large part of this market is undiscriminating but ready to part with hard cash—indeed, almost asking to be fooled.

Real old pewter consists of tin with small parts of lead and/or antimony. It will burnish to the colour of old silver, but of course many surving specimens have acquired the dull patination of age and it would be mistaken to remove this by polishing. The faker is helped in his work enormously as there is no impediment in law to prevent him from applying 'genuine' 'touch' marks to his products (as, for instance, he cannot do with silver).

'Touch' marks, it may be explained here, are the marks which were applied by means of punches to articles of pewter and sometimes of copper by, in Scotland, the Guilds of Hammermen, and in England the Pewterers Company. These 'touches' identify the maker by his mark and also give a guide to date, since most are traceable to their date of registration and of course the mark of the guild or company is also given. They are distinct from the revenue marks common on spirit measures which it is of course illegal to copy.

In passing, it might be noted that most fake marks on fake pewter are placed wrongly, i.e. where they are most easily seen, such as on the handle, but where in fact, if genuine, they would not be struck, since these are the places most subject to wear through use and polishing.

Ceramics

Undoubtedly the greatest market for the faker, however, is in the field of ceramics, for practically everyone likes to purchase an old piece of china at one time or another. In days past, when faking was largely confined to high quality and expensive porcelain, the firm of Samson in Paris turned out copies of an astonishingly high standard of every conceivable item from Ming vases to Meissen figures, complete with the correct marks of origin, and today the products of the Samson workshops command high prices in their own right.

Early earthenware, on the other hand, is rarely faked, since the market is so far too small and discriminating. Furthermore, eighteenth-century earthenware, with the exception of Delft, is rarely marked, and therefore real knowledge is required on the part of the collector and of the dealer in order to establish the provenance of each piece.

It is true that on the continent such tin-glazed earthenwares as Dutch Delft and Majolica are copied in great quantity, and these are bought and sold, to an extent at least in Britain, very often by those on both sides of the counter who should know better. On the other hand, a truly vast amount of pottery was produced in Britain from the 1830s onwards, much of it most colourful and appealing, but made on a mass-produced basis, which makes it extremely easy and cheap to produce today, using essentially the same materials and methods of Victorian factory production.

As a typical instance, 'Stafford' figures (they were, in fact, made all over Britain) are at present enjoying a tremendous vogue. The earliest of these figures, dating to the end of the eighteenth century, are quite diminutive in size and modelled all round, rather in the manner of their porcelain counterparts, although they have a freshness and vigour which is often quite absent from their rich relations.

As the nineteenth century progressed, these figures became larger and coarser, while the backs were hardly moulded at all and indeed are often completely devoid both of form and colour. The colours used were often vigorous and bold but coarsely applied and can therefore be easily faked. Unfortunately, this class of ware is widely collected and high, indeed ridiculously high, prices are paid for named specimens, that is, pieces such as 'Dick Turpin', 'Dr Palmer' and so on.

Some of the original moulds for this class of ware survive, and copies can be obtained 'in the white', to be decorated over-glaze and 're-cooked' in the amateur's kiln. Smaller wares, such as the famous 'Rockingham' pastille burners and banks, sheep and inkwells, have long been forged, and copies are at present reportedly being imported from Spain at a few shillings each.

The really enterprising dealer can help their appearance along by wetting a few and placing them in the dust bag of a vacuum cleaner, and then, after they have dried out, washing them, thus leaving the dust of ages in all the little crevices.

Lustre ware jugs, particularly of the copper coloured variety, are still widely made, and of course such items as frog mugs are so numerous in the shops that there must be at least 20 fakes on sale for each genuine article.

Avoiding Fakes

Now then, can one avoid falling for the spurious in the process of learning about the genuine article, or separating, as it were, the wheat from the chaff?

No amount of book reading or visits to museums, invaluable as these are, can be a substitute for the opportunity to handle the genuine item, and to check and observe, compare and discuss, which can only be done with a reputable dealer. At this point, I must stress several things. An experienced dealer is not necessarily expensive. He knows what price to pay for his goods and he is not such a fool as to drive away business by taking more than a reasonable profit. He will also welcome anyone who is keen and anxious to learn, partly because this is good long-term business policy but mainly because he is an enthusiast himself and his work is also his hobby.

Lastly and most important, any dealer worth his salt will 'stand by' his description of an article sold by him and return his customer's money without question should there be the slightest doubt of its authenticity. Indeed, over a period quite a bit of trading is transacted with dealer and customer in the reverse direction, i.e., as prices rise and should a customer wish to sell an article back, the dealer can often give his customer a profit on his original price.

So cultivate the friendship of a reliable dealer, and remember that in doing this, it is the man (or the woman) and his stock which count. For dealers are notoriously independent and even eccentric characters, so that while many beautifully laid-out shops look (and are) so expensive that one is intimidated from even entering them, a great many of this variety, even for instance in Bond Street, are surprisingly reasonable in their pricing, while others may be filled with expensive rubbish.

It can also be true that behind a higgledy-piggledy pile of goods there sits a man with real knowledge and erudition: not easy at first perhaps to come to terms with, but if he spots you as a genuine character, you have a friend as well as a dealer, the kind who will keep some items in a drawer until your next call and say, 'Now, I put this aside for I knew it would interest you as we were talking about . . .'

3   Inside the Sale-Room

Sources of Supply

A friend of mine in the antique trade has a notice displayed in his shop reading: 'We make a small charge for listening about the things your granny threw away.'

Like most dealers, my friend has suffered for years, not merely by listening to heartrending stories of 'fortunes' thrown into the ash bucket but also by having to explain in as kind a way as possible that the 'treasures' brought to him for valuation, '... which must be antique as they were left by my grandmother who was born in 1830 ...' are in fact some prized pieces of pottery bought by the same granny in Woolworths just before she died in 1920. Indeed a bitter pill to swallow.

The truth is that now most antiques coming on to the market do so in the normal process of re-distribution, just in the same way as secondhand cars or vacuum cleaners. Discoveries are made, of course, and constantly so, but these represent only a fraction of the amount of antiques the trade needs to turn over in order to survive.

Auction Sales

There are three main sources of supply for the dealer. In order of importance these are, generally speaking, auction sales, buying from the trade itself, and private treaty.

If one had a sensational turn of mind and a taste for muck-raking, possibly the easiest target for a best-seller or a Sunday paper 'exposé' would be auction sales.

Basically, the reason for this is the common practice of 'ringing', which, though highly illegal since 1927, still flourishes in auction rooms all over Britain. But 'ringing' is largely a scandal only because of a bad and unworkable law and is certainly no more scandalous than street bookmaking or prostitution were at the time when these business activities were hamstrung by unworkable legislation.

Under the Auctions (Bidding Agreements) Act of 1927, the forming of a 'ring', that is, a group of intending purchasers to act in secret in order to limit competition and thus keep down prices, is a felony. However, the 'ring' flourishes despite pious declarations from dealers and auctioneers to the contrary, and in practice works like this.

A group of dealers makes an informal agreement not to bid against each other, the composition of the group being fairly fluid from district to district. At the actual sale, one dealer will act as 'banker' and, while other dealers may appear to bid against each other, they are merely 'passing the ball' when outside bids have to be fended off. After the sale, the 'ring' then re-auction the goods they have purchased and the difference between 'their' price and the sale price of each lot is divided in a process known as a 'knock-out'.

Thus, if Lot No. 12 fetched £20 at the sale and it is 'knocked out' amongst a ring of four dealers, dealer A bids £24, which is £1 to each dealer in the ring, but dealer C bids him out at £30, which is a further £1.50 to each dealer in the ring, so that dealer C has got the lot for £27.50 and each 'ring' member has benefited by £2.50.

I do not myself purchase at auction sales and I have no particular brief for dealing of this kind, but, although it is illegal, I personally see nothing against a consortium of dealers, and certainly there is nothing to prevent outside dealers and private purchasers bidding against a 'ring'. In short, the Auction (Bidding Agreements) Act is a bad piece of law-making because it does not work, and a law which cannot be implemented brings the Law itself into disrepute. Worse than this, a bad law often serves to hide much more real abuses which the Law and an informed public opinion ought to tackle.

It is quite often the case that a dealer or a group of dealers will enter items for sale and 'trot them up' themselves, i.e., deliberately bid up the price against the private buyer.

While all auctioneers will accept private bids before the sale, it would be quite naive to expect these bids to remain secret until the article actually comes to offer. There are too many 'perks' to put in the way of auction room staff by dealers and dealers' rings to expect private bids to remain private, unless of course these concern important lots at a few leading salerooms.

The 'quick knock' is prevalent at many salerooms, mostly the smaller variety, but certainly by no means confined to them. This is trade slang for an auctioneer who can, when he chooses, 'knock down' quickly, without the remark, 'Going, going, etc.', and by possibly going blind to another bid just for the required second or two. Any bid at dispute in a saleroom must by law be resolved by exposing the goods concerned for re-auction. Perhaps a determined exercise of their rights by the public attending auctions would stop many of the abuses which do not bring credit to the business of public auctioneer.

These criticisms I have made are essentially criticisms of a system, i.e., the system of auction by open competitive bidding, and no criticism of the profession of auctioneer is intended, which profession has its share of honourable men, just as any other: doctors, lawyers, even antique dealers!

Buying within the Trade

The antiques trade is, above all things, a sifting process. Dealer A has an item which dealer B thinks he can sell to dealer C, who in turn knows a collector who is looking for such a piece. Under these conditions, it is inevitable that a vast amount of buying and selling is done within the trade, and for this reason any experienced dealer regards other dealers not as competitors but as friends, and the more antique shops in an area, the better it is for everyone concerned.

Most of my own buying is done from the trade, and I find that this is a satisfactory method of buying, both from an economic standpoint and also because it is stimulating and satisfying in a way that buying at auction can never be. Buying from the trade, one develops a keen sense of value, based on the intrinsic merits of an item rather than the mechanical method of bidding at auction, and at the same time there is always the thrill of discovery insofar as a gap in the knowledge of another dealer can lead to a real bargain in the particular field in which one has a specialized knowledge.

When I talk of a 'gap' in knowledge on the part of a dealer, I do not mean this in any disparaging way. No dealer is an expert in every field. I have given some resounding bargains, unwittingly at the time, to dealers who remain my good friends. Why not? They are entitled to the fruits of their knowledge.

Before I dealt in silver, I sold a pair of cast candlesticks (London 1743) for £225—about one fifth of their current value. Result: I started a serious study of silver. I also once sold a William and Mary embroidery for £1! Result: a close study of needlework. Only recently a dealer friend bought a teapot marked 'E.P.' as electroplate for £1.50. But the 'E.P.' stood for Edward Penman, Assay Master at Edinburgh, c. 1718!

Deals between dealers are fair game provided no dishonest statements are made by either party. But the layman selling to a dealer is entitled to special consideration. It is very true, and I know from experience, that the real finds to be made in antiques are much more often to be made in antique shops themselves rather than in private homes and salerooms.

Of course the occasional coup is merely the leaven in the bread, but its possibility does lead to a sharpening of the senses and at the same time to a broadening of knowledge, in which process some knowledge of, combined with a feeling for, history can be a priceless asset.

At this stage perhaps it should be stressed that by and large, the popular idea of an antique dealer working on minimum profit margins of 100 per cent is so much poppycock. Apart from the odd lucky strike, the experienced dealer will work on the tiniest of margins, i.e., gross margins of 10 per cent or even 5 per cent provided he sees a quick turnover in any item. This brings me to the last method of antique buying, which is by private treaty.

Buying by Private Treaty

Before antiques sold privately even reach a shop, they are often sold to a 'knocker'. These characters can range from the local rag-and-bone man to someone who has real knowledge and expertise. Of course, the knocker, whether he happens to be a scrap metal dealer who picks up the odd grandfather clock on the side, or the dealer who advertises that he will pay 'colossal prices' or who even masquerades as a 'private collector' or 'Buying Agent for American Lady', or whatever, will usually buy for as little as he possibly can. On the other hand, the 'knocker' will, if circumstances force him to, pay a very fair price indeed and in addition he pays immediately and in cash. Every dealer likes the prospect of a private buy when someone walks into his shop with something to sell on the invitation to call at his house.

Unfortunately, it is increasingly difficult to make a really good buy in this way, partly due to diminishing supply but mainly as a by-product of press, radio and television features on antiques, which tend to give the impression that antiques are largely things which are lying about unnoticed in the odd corners of umpteen thousand houses.

The result of all this is a constant procession of people going round and round antique shops with some china which 'must' be Meissen as it bears a mark with crossed swords, 'Delft'—a souvenir of some trip to Holland, 'silver' which is electroplate and every conceivable variety of cheap oriental brass and china. It is very difficult indeed to convince these hopefuls that what they have has probably a little value, one or two pounds at most, as these goods are consigned to what the trade calls the 'shipping end', that is, the large volume of goods bought in bulk, rather than by the item, and which is shipped abroad (not merely to the USA).

My own way out of this difficulty is perhaps the coward's one. I thank the caller for showing me the goods and suggest that as they are not my special field and of little value to me, he take them to another dealer. In this way, I may lose a pound or two but at least I do not gain the reputation of being a Shylock, always out to trap the innocent poor and occasionally, just occasionally, someone comes in with a really nice saleable item for which I am only too happy to give a fair price.

Selling to Dealers

What help then can I offer to those with antiques to sell? My first and most emphatic advice is, if you have something really nice, which you

15

like to live with and you are not desperate for the money, pay a reputable dealer his modest fee for a valuation, which is, remember, the price he would be prepared to spend on purchase at the present state of the market, then hold on to your treasure and enjoy your appreciating investment, which will give you, if you are a normal person, much more pleasure than depreciating currency in the bank.

However, assuming that you need the money, you should go to your dealer and explain that you intend to sell. Ask him to make a note of what he would offer you but also tell him not to name the figure as you intend to get another offer. Then, once you have obtained your offer elsewhere, you will come back and ask your first dealer to give you his.

Every dealer has constant and bitter experience of giving a good offer for some item only to have the seller go round the corner and say, 'Mr So-and-so has just offered me £50, so that you can have it for £52.

On the other hand, there is an unfortunate class of dealer who conducts business by demanding what price the seller has in mind, and then haggles on this basis; a procedure which is perfectly acceptable between dealers or between dealer and knowledgeable collector, but most definitely unfair to the average layman.

Advice from Museums

At this point I feel I must bring in the role of museums and art galleries in identifying antiques and works of art. Most national museums and galleries undertake this work, usually without fee but, of course, they will under no circumstances give valuations. The identification by museums is usually accurate but since it is not concerned with value, its practical application can be very misleading.

A stoneware bottle can be genuinely seventeenth century, for instance, but it may have little or no value. Only recently, I had the impossible task of explaining to a lady, who arrived in my shop with a genuine sixteenth-century German alms plate and a letter of identification (identifying the plate, of course, not the lady!) from a major museum, that her plate was worthless to me because she had removed the patination by burnishing it back and front with metal polish and steel wool and had pierced two large holes in the rim so that she could hang it on her wall.

Selling by Auction

The alternative method of disposing of antiques is through auction, the hazards of which I have described, but, provided one takes the

16

precaution of placing a reserve price (for which a commission will have to be paid up to the value of the bids received) and provided, once more, a reputable firm is used, there is no reason why a fair price cannot be obtained.

It is best to remember, however, that the major London houses will accept only top quality items for inclusion in their sales and that the process of selling, involving cataloguing and all its attendant planning, may take many months, so that more than half a year may elapse from acceptance of your goods to the receipt of your cheque.

Finally, one last observation, do not try to place a value on what you have to sell by comparison with similar items priced in glossy trade magazines or by the rather snide method of pricing what appears to be the same in a shop.

There are too many pitfalls here. The piece you compare may have a special feature, it may be grossly over-priced as a result of a dealer's bad buy, or the dealer may be just plain smarter than you think when you ask the price.

4   Picking the Genuine Article

I am often asked how I know an article is genuine and not a very good copy of what it purports to be. This is not an easy question to answer for most people concerned professionally with appraising antiques seem to arrive at their decisions instinctively. But is it instinct?

I think there is really a great deal of analytical knowledge involved, which has been called upon so many times that it no longer requires a series of questions and answers to determine whether a piece is right or not. However these questions and answers are there and I think, with all antiques, they fall into three separate categories: style and function; workmanship; materials.

Style and Function

A knowledge of history gives us our judgment on both style and function. We know, for instance, just when tea and chocolate became popular beverages and, therefore, just when teapots and chocolate pots began to be made. We also know that tea was once a great luxury and early teapots, in consequence, are bound to be small. We further know that various styles denote different ages, that the rococo replaced the baroque and was in turn displaced by the neo-classical, while the Victorian epoch imitated them all—but so badly that it is in itself a characteristic.

Workmanship

In terms of workmanship, early silver for example will be cast or 'raised' from a single sheet, while after about 1775 it will frequently be of thin sheets shaped by stamping or spinning on a lathe, with the resultant seams brazed together. Early pewter will be cast and hammered and much heavier than later copies, while pottery figures made before 1740 will not have been formed by moulding, as the process was only introduced from France about then.

Materials

Dealing with materials, we would not expect to find any British-made mahogany furniture before 1730 at the earliest, and no earthenware prior to about 1750 would have a white-coloured body with a

18

transparent glaze.

These are just a very few of the many thousands of factors which may at any time be used in arriving at a judgment. There is one more: the signs of genuine age.

Signs of Genuine Age

I have heard it said by a cynic in the trade that patination is just an expensive name for dirt. Be that as it may, patination, the surface effects of age, should always be present on genuinely old articles on those surfaces which have been exposed to the effects of light and the abrasive wear of polishing. By the same token—and this is where imitators often slip up—surfaces which are protected from these effects should be fresh, even pristine in appearance.

I would expect sharp hallmarks on the inside of the lid of a silver teapot, for instance. Similarly the underside of a drawer on a piece of furniture, while it may be, and indeed should be, scratched by the constant opening and shutting, will at the same time be of raw and unstained wood.

To illustrate what I have been saying, it might be worth while examining the cabinet shown here. This is of walnut veneer and was originally on top of a stand which has, sadly, been lost.

The idea of these cabinets was that with their useful drawers and pigeon holes, they would act as a 'secretary'; this, in fact, was what they were called. The style is typical of the late seventeenth century, and by about 1700 the bureau as we know it had arrived. This, of course, had a sloping top which dropped to form a writing surface and which, when closed, concealed all the storage space.

While walnut was known and used in the solid both in this country and in Holland, it was not used as a veneer until the second half of the seventeenth century. The idea of veneers is to bring out the beauty of the wood grain by cutting thin slabs particularly where the grain is nicely figured and glueing these slabs on to a carcase commonly of oak or pine. All early veneers were cut by hand, and as a very rough guide the older they are the thicker they are. Thicknesses of up to an eighth of an inch are known, and this particular piece has veneers of about one tenth.

These thicknesses can be observed at the edges of the doors and the sides of the drawers. Machine-cut veneers, whether Victorian or modern, just do not have the appearance of the hand-cut variety.

Much late-seventeenth-century furniture is inlaid, either in the form of marquetry—floral arrangements being favourite—or simply by narrow bands of another wood such as yew or mulberry or even oak. This is known as 'stringing' and our cabinet is decorated in this way.

19

It is a curious fact that even although much furniture styling of this period is originally Dutch, the English inlay work is invariably of better quality. This superior workmanship is the main way of determining whether a particular piece is English or Dutch.

Looking beneath the veneer, all the main joints will be by mortice and tenon (or 'tenant' as the word originally was), that is a 'tongue' of wood fitting into a slot and secured by a willow peg driven into a hole

Secretary, open.

in both pieces. In veneered furniture this peg is covered, but where it is present and visible in genuine old furniture, such as an oak cupboard or table, it will, due to the gradual shrinkage of the surrounding wood, stand up 'proud'—a very handy point to check.

The drawers in our secretary are fastened by dovetail joints both back and front. In a Dutch piece they would probably be 'butted up' at the ends and secured by nails and glue. Dovetailing only developed during the seventeenth century and at first the actual cuts made to form the dovetail shape were very large indeed.

It should also be noted that until mid-century these cuts came through to the front of the wood so that they were visible from all angles, and for the larger joints at least this practice often continued

20

for some years, and indeed is the case at the top of our cabinet.

The furnishings of our piece, the metal handles and hinges, are largely original. The hinges for the main doors have worn and been replaced.

A glance at the screw heads tells me they are fairly modern as the cuts to take the screwdriver are dead centre and not slightly off centre as they always are on hand-cut screws. If I took out one of the screws I

Secretary, closed.

would find that it was pointed, which it should not be, and that the spiral was cut much less obliquely than on a hand-made screw.

The drawer handles, however, are original: nice little tear drops in brass with rosettes behind them and fastened at the back with iron split pins, just as they should be until about 1690. Pleasant strap hinges of steel hold the inside of the small door in the centre.

Most of these cabinets had more drawers than is apparent, and this is no exception. There is a nest of drawers behind the door in the centre, and that solid-looking cornice conceals a large drawer. By

21

pulling on the sides of the pigeon holes, yet more secret drawers are exposed.

I wish I could say that the outside surfaces of the drawer bottoms and sides are of raw wood as they should be. Unfortunately some past do-it-yourself enthusiast has stained some of them a dark colour.

However, their other characteristics remain: they are scored beneath where they have been continually drawn over nails and other slight projections in the carcase and, a strange thing, the wood of the drawer bottoms runs from back to front, and not from side to side. It has always rather puzzled me why drawers made before about 1740 should be constructed in this way but it is a point to note, and while there are exceptions to the rule they are few indeed.

One last thing remains: I look at my cabinet and it is obvious that it has 'settled' into its present comfortable old age. All wood is subject to stresses, to shrinkage and to distortion, and over a long period of time this process works its way until all the pulls and pressures have accommodated themselves.

My cabinet has gone through this process. It has learned about all there is to know of life and now it can comfortably relax—which, come to think of it, having seen the first light of day about the same time as King Billy came to British shores, it is well entitled to do.

5   Investing in Furniture

One commonly held misconception, no doubt fostered by the advertisements of some dealers, is that most of the antiques shipped from this country are destined for the United States. While it is true that the U.S. is an important buyer of antiques—and of what passes as antique—it has now to take its place in the queue with the Germans, the Dutch, the Swedes and the Italians—and even such unlikely buyers as Icelanders, Finns and Mexicans. 'Everyone', as Jimmy Durante once remarked, 'wants to get in on the act.'

I recently spent a hectic week playing my own small part in this export drive by taking an Italian dealer friend, complete with very large truck, around antique furniture dealers in Scotland and the North of England. It certainly gave me food for thought: while truly colossal quantities of Georgian and Victorian furniture are being shipped out of this country, I am constantly surprised by the amount which remains, much of it moderately priced.

I know that for most people, furnishing a house, or even adding a piece or two, often means hire purchase. But surely, if necessary with the aid of a loan, more use could be made of antique furniture as part of a practical furnishing scheme. Apart from its often surprising cheapness, it does not depreciate in value and, indeed, is likely to be a sound investment.

Real Value

Value is, of course, difficult to assess, and I suppose old Karl Marx was about the only person to claim to do this with any degree of exactitude, but my own method is simply to look at something and ask myself just what it would cost to reproduce it. The value of this approach is that it eliminates to a very large degree the element of fashion and concentrates instead on materials and workmanship.

To take an example: if I look at the very fashionable and attractive little table called a sofa table—that is, a table oblong in shape which may be supported by a variety of pillars, but always with two leaves hanging from the narrow ends—I see a piece of furniture which fashion has made much too dear. For a good sofa table I would be asked to pay from £300 to £600.

On the other hand, for a good quality small table with a fold-over top and four legs made about 1790, I would not expect to pay much

23

over £90 and for the same style of top on a single pedestal dating 40 to 50 years later, my price would range from about £50 to £80.

Still on tables, I can buy retail an excellent Georgian Pembroke style; this means four legs on an oblong top with leaves on either side but hung on the broad sides. Provded it is not richly inlaid the price will still be nearer £50 than £80. If I prefer a similar top but on a single pedestal base, then I could pay as little as £40 for a good specimen made about 1840.

All of these tables are neat in size, of excellent workmanship and most attractive. In addition, they make ideal tables for four, or six when opened out—something for which the sofa table is quite unsuited.

At the prices I have quoted, one is buying cheaply in the best sense of that misused word, and apart from the fact that modern reproductions could not be made for anything like these modest sums, the quality of the woods used, both in carcase and veneers, is much better than those available to today's workmen.

If you want to go backwards in time and consider the furniture available from the late seventeenth and early eighteenth century, you can still buy a piece of furniture which is functional and at the same time a fascinating piece of history. Most surviving furniture from this period is of oak, although some walnut, particularly in the form of chairs, is not too difficult to find.

When buying oak furniture, however, you must be fairly careful, for much was produced during the mid-Victorian period. With some exceptions, this reproduction oak is over-decorated with fussy carving and stained a treacly dark colour, which is no doubt the reason it is often referred to in the trade as 'boarding house Gothic'.

Oak Furniture

Oak furniture when it was made was left quite 'raw', and the real stuff today has acquired its mellow appearance through ages of wear and polishing. Any genuine old furniture, indeed, is quite new and fresh looking on those surfaces not exposed to wear and to daylight, and for this reason it is always a good plan to inspect such places as the insides of drawers.

In the seventeenth and early eighteenth centuries, furniture was joined together by means of a 'tongue' of wood on one piece, fitting a groove on the other, and secured by a willow peg driven through a hole in both tongue and groove. Over the years the carcase has contracted slightly, leaving the pegs lying a little way above the surface and this can quite easily be seen or even felt with the palm of the hand. Dovetailing, such as at the fronts of drawers, will be much wider than

24

Oak chest of drawers with typical brass pear-drop handles. Made about 1660.

Dower Chest of about 1700, inlaid oak, fitted with two drawers.

one usually sees and on earlier pieces will come right through to the exposed fronts.

These are just a few simple points to watch for, but, of course, with the price range of furniture we are discussing, faking is not an important factor.

Most early oak tables of the refectory type are, needless to say, much too large for the average modern house. However, a surprising number of smaller tables have survived in oak, many of which were originally designed as side tables; 'sideboards' in fact.

The larger of these make splendid dining tables and the very small ones have a variety of self-evident uses. They fit in almost anywhere and apart from their mellow, warm appearance they have the inestimable virtue of being so robustly constructed as to be virtually indestructible. Again the price range is usually well under the £150 mark, and although this represents a considerable recent increase, prices are certain to rise higher yet again.

Oak chests, usually referred to as dower chests, have survived in considerable numbers, and to my mind these represent one of the very best buys available today. Most date from the mid-seventeenth century until about 100 years later. They are simply constructed of oaken planks, sometimes with some carving and often with the addition of inlay in yew, holly, or later, mahogany.

These later ones have two drawers at the foot; embryonic chests of drawers in fact, fitted with heavy brass lockplates and handles. Quite the most useful type of furniture for a hall or, indeed, for any part of the house, they are interesting to look at and will hold all sorts of odds and ends. Yet these genuine early chests start in price at about £50 and rarely go above £100 for the very best examples.

Apart from considerations of price, attractiveness and above all, of course, of sheer usefulness, everything I describe in this book will fit into any kind of home and blend happily with almost all types of furniture.

6 Sitting on a Bargain

Chairs

I have already discussed some items of antique furniture which remain cheaper than the reproduced article but I have not as yet mentioned chairs.

The other night when eating out at the house of friends, I was reminded just what kind of bargains one could once come across. This couple had bought a lovely set of four mahogany sabre legged Georgian chairs some ten years ago for exactly ten shillings each. At that time, of course, it was difficult to sell chairs unless they were in sets of six, and no doubt the dealer sighed with relief when he got rid of a 'sticker'.

In a sense, the same sort of situation appertains today. Often on my rounds I see excellent singles or doubles and even trebles of good

Early Victorian fold-over table—pictured opened out as small dining table—and Victorian 'balloon-back' chairs.

Georgian and Victorian chairs, for only two, three or four pounds a chair. Odd chairs are, after all, always wanted in a house and it is not too difficult to assemble sets from twos and threes which are almost matching, and certainly close enough for those occasions when they all need to be assembled together at the one time.

The classic Georgian chair is of mahogany with two spars running across the back, sabre-shaped legs back and front, and with a seat that lifts out. Coming into the nineteenth century, the front legs become turned and straight, but the rear legs remain sabre-shaped. Later still the shape of the back is that of a balloon outline, either 'full' or sagging at the middle; the seat becomes a fixture, the legs are now straight and

Preceding table in closed position.

turned or cabriole-shaped at the front, and mahogany sometimes gives way to rosewood or walnut.

Three things all of these chairs have in common: pleasing shapes, excellence of materials, and fine workmanship. Fairly high prices are now being paid for sets of good chairs, especially if they have carvers, and even fours fetch good money. It is only a matter of time, and in my estimation not very much time, before dealers start furiously searching around for the hitherto neglected odd numbers.

I have previously mentioned earlier examples of furniture, particularly in oak, and it is quite remarkable that really early chairs in this wood are not at all difficult to find. The best of these are from the seventeenth century and have very high and straight backs. Legs, stretchers and splats are usually turned in the 'barley sugar' manner of the period, and the backs are normally carved with crowns or shells.

These chairs come in walnut as well as oak, and the latter often have cane seats and back panels. Once more, while sets of these early chairs are rare, single examples, ideal for hall or bedroom, can easily be found. Prices are seldom over £25, and often much less.

One of life's mysteries is that I can go to an auction sale, or pick up a trade paper, and note that much higher prices are being paid for antique furniture there than for similar pieces available in dealers' shops. A case in point is the chest of drawers.

Chests of Drawers

The chest of drawers gradually emerged from the oaken dower chest by the addition of drawers at the foot. The next step was the provision of more drawers so that the top could be left closed, and the internal space conveniently utilized.

This change took place in the middle of the seventeenth century, and although the recent interest in early oak has sent the prices of these very early chests of drawers soaring, it is interesting that they can still be found in some shops at around the £100 mark—much less than they fetch at auction. I am describing the solid oak variety, of course, as inlaid work will always be dearer.

There are, however, several features that make oak chests most attractive, apart from the warm patination of the wood. They are usually quite small and often they consist of two sections, one lying on top of the other.

This construction made it easy to negotiate winding staircases, and it is equally handy in modern conditions. The fronts, too, are built up around the drawers and the frame with a combination of split bobbin work and geometric panels which are quite distinctive. The iron handles will be either ring or pear-shaped, secured with a split pin at the back. A little later the handles will become brass.

This business of handles, by the way, is a very handy guide to dating any chest apart from the methods of construction which I have described. Pear drop handles give way first to solid, then to pierced, brass escutcheon plates; later to plates of thin stamped brass; and finally to the Victorian wooden 'bun' variety. You must always check, of course, that the handles are original before passing judgment.

Later chests of drawers, from about 1740, were usually made of mahogany. Apart from the finest specimens and those with serpentine-shaped fronts, you could, until recently, have picked up any amount of these for as little as £10—and seldom more than £40.

Buyers from abroad, however, have been riding heavily on this particular bandwagon and in general the bargains have gone. I still see quite a few late Georgian chests, plain fronted but with nice handles and cock beaded round the drawers; in solid mahogany or veneered on to a pine carcase, they are priced at £45 to £70 and they are very good value.

It is always worth remembering that these early veneers were hand cut and therefore much thicker than those available today; this means greater durability.

Woodworm

And do not allow a few worm holes to deter you from buying. Worms like their food soft, and will eat the hardwoods only when they are stuck for a meal; in any event, it is unusual to find live worm in old furniture. A tap with a hard object on the surface will, if the worm is active, send little puffs of dust out of the holes. If this simple test is negative, there is nothing to worry about.

It is not possible in this context to give a blow-by-blow account of every item of antique furniture which remains underpriced. Good old pine pieces, for instance, remain fairly plentiful, some much older than a superficial glance suggests.

The Italians, with their innate sense of style, are busy cutting and adapting all sorts of British late Victorian furniture, which is much too massive for modern use. At the same time, they are happily using un-altered such items as chiffoniers, made in great numbers around the 1850s in quite small and neat sizes, and largely scorned by the home market. Commodes, both Georgian and Victorian, make ideal drinks cabinets, and tiled washstands which the trade once could not even give away are now used as bedroom and occasional tables.

7   A Day's Buying

Britain is still, despite years of exporting, an incredibly rich country in terms of the quantity and sheer diversity of the antiques to be found in it, sometimes in the most unlikely areas.

Thus it was that recently I was very pleasantly surprised to be shown a small sixteenth-century Italian cassone in a country antique shop in North-west England. I was even more pleasantly surprised to hear the modest price of just over two figures quoted to me and I am now the possessor of a lovely little specimen of one of the earliest and most popular pieces of furniture to have survived what Victorian novelists were fond of calling 'the ravages of time'.

Basically all European furniture has evolved from the bed and the chest. There is little that time and taste could do with the first except make it a little more comfortable, but the chest was father to both the table and the chair, and by itself it gradually evolved, by the addition of drawers and height, into both the wardrobe and chest of drawers, and later into the bureau and the bookcase.

In northern Europe, the chest was usually of oak and because this wood is hard and straight-grained, and because northern Europe at that time was a pretty rough place, it was made with only the simplest of carving.

These oak chests, by the way, are still quite easily found. Good specimens from the seventeenth and early eighteenth century still sell for £50 to £100 or so, even if prices are rapidly rising with the renewed popularity of oak. Heavy carving should be avoided, particularly carved mounts, as this was commonly done in the late nineteenth century, thus ruining genuine pieces.

In Italy, chests, or cassoni, as they are called, were made of fruitwood, particularly walnut, and were richly carved, as my chest is, usually because they were marriage gifts bearing conjoined coats of arms. Walnut is a lovely wood but, unlike oak, it makes an ideal abode for worms. Still, I suppose the worms who ate their way through my cassone were of the very best class.

Also from Italy came eighteenth-century carved pine torchères in the form of a Blackamoor gorgeously attired in turban and gilded robe, and originally holding aloft a multi-coloured glass torch from Murano. Early-nineteenth-century versions of these were made both in England and the United States, often by ships' carvers, and to my mind they are much more attractive, as they are smaller and they have an unsophisticated spontaneity which their Venetian counterparts lack.

My find, in the same shop as the cassone, had been dreadfully mutilated in the late nineteenth-century by some clown who had taken off the tray held in the hand of the kneeling Blackamoor, and replaced it with the seat of a piano stool! It was now just the thing for some bizarre establishment in Chelsea but not, I reflected, for me.

This example of an Italian cassone, or chest, probably belongs to the mid-sixteenth century. They are always made of fruitwood, usually walnut.

At home that night, however, it struck me that it would not be at all difficult to have the piano stool top removed and by having a mahogany tray made re-convert the torchère to its original function. I phoned the dealer, therefore, and made arrangements to call and collect the following week.

Now comes the saddest part of my story, for on entering the dealer's shop a week later, I noticed three pieces of scrimshaw work displayed in the window.

Scrimshaw is the name given to ivory, engraved lightly by seamen (usually in the whaling trade) and mainly during the nineteenth century. The ivory used is usually, although not invariably, sea ivory —that is, walrus or narwhal tusks or the teeth of the killer whale. Scrimshaw work often depicts whaling or other sea-going activities and sometimes romantic themes, and these particular pieces interested me for two reasons.

The first reason for particular interest was that all three pieces had on them engravings of a Jacobite theme—Prince Charles Edward Stuart, crossed broadswords, white cockades and so on. My second reason for interest was that they had been offered to me a couple of weeks before by a dealer who, in response to my question as to their authenticity, assured me that they were genuine as he had made them himself.

My English friend, by no means an unknowledgeable man, had bought the scrimshaw in good faith, not from the crook who offered the pieces to me, but at one remove. Since scrimshaw can fetch over £100 for one good piece, my friend, a scrupulously honest man, stood to lose a fair sum of money. This is, I suppose, where antique dealing has just that additional element of chance to it—more so than many other ways of making a living.

8 How to Turn an Oak Bureau into a Walnut Masterpiece

I found my bureau in a corner of farm stables. Like the stables themselves, the bureau had been abandoned for more modern things. Modern ploughing and carting is done by tractor and agricultural accounts are filed neatly in metal cabinets.

For me, however, there is nothing quite like a bureau for storing bills and receipts, odd bits of string, fishing tackle and in fact anything which is liable to be handy—but not just yet. A bureau will take enormous quantities of the most varied articles in its drawers and pigeon holes. You can then close the whole thing up and presto, the room looks tidy.

My bureau had undoubtedly seen better days and those days had begun just about the time Queen Anne was getting seriously worried about her weight. It was of oak, with a little inlay of yew wood on the flap: one thing about oak—short of hitting it with an axe, it is practically indestructible. Most furniture in Britain, from the late seventeenth and early eighteenth centuries, was made of oak and that is why such a remarkable amount of it has survived.

By the end of the seventeenth century, however, the new-fangled walnut had already arrived on the scene and this was used as a veneer on top of an oak, or sometimes a pine carcase. Used in this way, walnut gave a most beautiful effect but it was expensive, fashionable and very easily damaged. Particularly in country areas, therefore, oak remained firm favourite for many years to come.

I paid the farmer £75 for the bureau and together we hoisted it on top of the car. We were both, I am sure, happy with the bargain. To him the money was found, and I reckoned that I could get about £100 for it even unrestored. Not, as I saw when I had the time to examine it thoroughly, that there was much damage.

Apart from neglect, there was really very little to complain about. The bracket feet seemed original and so were the heavy brass handles and escutcheons. The interior, always an important point with a bureau, was very pretty, being built up of little scallop-fronted drawers and pigeon holes.

The typical 'secret' cavity was no longer very secret as wear around the edges readily revealed its presence. Miraculously, all the little brass drawer pulls were still *in situ* and I felt very pleased.

No African tribe ever developed a bush telegraph to the level of efficiency common in the antique business. So it was that on the next day but one I received a telephone call from a London dealer enquiring about my bureau. I knew the dealer only slightly, but he obviously knew my bureau just as well as I did for I had no need to describe it to him. All he wanted was my price and so long as that was realistic, he wished to buy it.

I was on the point of quoting my figure of £100 to him when something made me hesitate. 'Look,' I said, 'I have a private customer waiting for an early oak bureau and I have promised him first refusal.

Typical early-eighteenth-century bureau, showing interior.

I'll ring you if it doesn't suit him. But you are a walnut and mahogany man; oak isn't of much interest to you.'

There was the merest pause at the other end of my line: 'I would very much like it. I have a private customer also who wants to buy an oak bureau.'

I am not by nature a suspicious character but the London dealer is the kind who scorns humble oak, no matter how genuine. 'Now walnut,' I thought, 'if that bureau was walnut I could understand it. An early walnut bureau, nice interior, small size, original condition, that would be worth at least £600 in the trade.'

The penny dropped all of a sudden, as pennies do. If this dealer were

Heavy dovetail joints were a feature of early drawer construction.

to clad my oak bureau in walnut veneer as a really skilled restorer could do, he could increase its value something like five-fold. Modern veneers would, of course, be of little use. They have no colour and would easily betray themselves by their paper thinness. Hand-cut veneers can still be made, but best of all are veneers from irreparably-broken old items of furniture such as chests and tallboys and even the odd Georgian square piano.

Given the proper treatment, it would be a very sharp person—be he dealer or private buyer—who would spot anything wrong. The carcase, after all, was completely right. The usual elementary tests would show that.

The grain of the wood in the drawers ran the right way, from back to front. The wearmarks on the foot of the drawers corresponded with the wearmarks on the carcase and they were constructed correctly for the period; big dovetails at the front and hand-made nails at the backs. The oaken back boards were original, nailed on with big, hand-made nails and unstained.

The interior was exactly right and even the handles were as they should be. If the patination were carefully removed from the veneer at precisely the right places, before the handles were re-affixed, this, perhaps the most crucial part of the job, would be well-nigh undetectable. And, of course, a really top craftsman would use animal glues to apply his veneers.

I could imagine the dealer with his prospective customer: 'Yes, madam, this is a genuine period bureau, Queen Anne or George First at the latest. You have my guarantee on that. Of course, madam, I will in all honesty point out that there has been some restoration. On a piece such as this, one must expect wear consistent with what is, after all, a very early bureau. However, where veneer has had to be restored it has been done with the utmost care and matching materials of the same age.'

I had been speaking the truth when I told the dealer that I had a private customer for the bureau. That evening I telephoned him and gave him a description. My customer was very interested.

'Do you think', he said when I pointed out that it required some restoration, 'that I could do the work on it myself.'

'For a handyman like you', I assured him, 'there should be no problem.'

9   Buying Time

Many years ago, in company with a few thousand other reluctant heroes, I found myself undertaking a long sea voyage in the North Atlantic. From the blunt end to the sharp end the ship, a large and ancient Dutch East Indiaman, was crammed with bodies in ill-fitting khaki, my own particular berth being a very small corner of what had once been the swimming pool. The name of that ship was the *Christiaan Huygens,* and it is a name which I am sure is remembered without regret by the many thousands of unfortunates she carried on those war-time voyages.

To the Dutch, however, the name of Huygens will always be remembered as that of the physicist who, in the year 1656, first fitted a pendulum to a clock and as a result produced for the first time a clock whose accuracy could be relied on.

All clocks before this period were shockingly bad time-keepers. As they relied on the energy of a compressed spring to drive them, the force of the spring diminished as the clock wound down, so that there was no way to regulate the escapement evenly. The great Galileo had, of course, discovered the principle of the pendulum, by observing that the swinging lamps in the cathedral at Pisa took exactly the same time to perform their arc, whether it was a wide or a narrow one.

The contribution Christiaan Huygens made was to apply the principle of the pendulum in a practical way, so that the escaping energy of a spring-driven clock, or the deadweight of a weight-driven clock, could be regulated.

Since the pendulum, many other improvements have marked the progress of watch and clock making. The escapement mounted on the edge or the 'verge' has given way to the much simpler and more accurate 'anchor' escapement shaped exactly as its name suggests. Another invention, the 'fusee', was of particular value to the mechanisms of small clocks and watches.

The fusee is basically another way of regulating the escaping energy of the spring, by attaching the escapement via a cord or chain to a cone-shaped piece of brass. The drive begins at the narrow part of the cone and unwinds downwards, so that as the energy of the spring diminishes, the greater amount of the fusee is unwound by the given degree of pressure, thus making the escapement an even quantity.

From the period marked by the restoration of Charles II, to the early nineteenth century, English, and later British, clock-making was

39

English 'Lantern' clock of about 1670.

Typical Black Forest wall clock of about 1820.

French 'Comtoise' clock with verge escapement dated 1812.

supreme. Some very fine work was done on the Continent, of course, particularly in the Jura region both of France and Switzerland, but the richness and variety of British clocks and watches is astonishing; so too is the sheer quantity that must have been made.

It is not here my intention to enthuse further on the common or 'Grandfather' clock. It is, however, worth mentioning that very early examples from about 1700 to 1730 made outside London, and usually with an hour hand only, are still very cheap to buy from £50 to £90 or so.

This is the style of clock I have at home, our own particular example hailing from Dublin and dating from about 1675. The face is so clearly marked with quarter hour divisions that I can set my wrist watch by it—which, after 300 years, is, I think, some form of poetic justice.

Clocks from the seventeenth century such as the lantern type shown here are necessarily expensive (that is, about the price of a decent second-hand car but a much better investment), but wall and mantel clocks from the late eighteenth century can be found on the right side of £100, particularly if no London maker is involved.

In the early nineteenth century, clock pedlars from the Black Forest region of Germany made their appearance in Britain. The clocks they sold were simple, driven by pendulum and weights with brightly-painted wooden faces and even, sometimes, with wooden movements.

These clocks are remarkably robust, as witnessed by the many thousands still ticking merrily away after 150-odd years. Like all good things, they have risen in price lately, but they can still be found from £25 to £30. The Black Forest clocks, for all their cheapness, were hand-made in the winter by the same peasants who in summer hawked them for sale as far afield as Scotland and Russia.

In 1842 an American, Chauncey Jerome, sent a consignment of his new factory-made clocks to England. The British Customs promptly impounded the lot and paid for their invoiced value, as was their right to do when they considered that there had been an attempt to cheat the revenue by understating the value of the goods.

Jerome was, of course, delighted to sell his shipment so quickly, and before long his clocks, very cheap, reliable eight-day movements encased in glass, were flooding the British market.

These typical rectangular American clocks, either spring or weight-driven with a glass door and a pasted-on notice explaining how the clock was to be set up and adjusted, at one time took pride of place beside the white earthenware 'wally dugs' in just about every farm cottage in Scotland. Many of them, I trust and hope, still do.

Four years ago, I was buying them when I could, against much shaking of heads by older dealers, for three pounds each. Recently I could still get them at £10 and now I have managed to buy a few at £15. I did see a specimen in London recently, priced at £65, and I suppose that in a year or so that will not seem so wildly improbable a price.

Some of the best French movements were encased in marble or slate to form mantel clocks and these I used to buy for half a crown. They are still cheap, from £10 to £20. The splendid, heavily jewelled movements would cost the earth to make today, but there was little demand abroad, as the clocks were expensive to ship. In any case, mantelpieces had gone out of fashion.

Clocks are wonderful things: they combine history, craftsmanship and utility. There is nothing quite like the friendly sound of an old clock ticking away in the hall or by the fireplace; they are, indeed, one of the things that go to make a real home.

10 Anatomy of a Swindle

Most antique dealers are honest, as honest indeed as the average citizen, and you can read into that anything you wish. Some antique dealers, however, are dishonest and like the little boy who was not merely bad but horrid, these dishonest dealers try not to miss a trick.

The latest and most profitable swindle concerns that most familiar and enduring staple of the antique trade, the 'Grandfather' or 'long-case' clock.

Since the year 1656, when the Dutchman Christiaan Huygens first applied the principle of the pendulum in order to regulate efficiently the timing mechanism of a clock, thousands and thousands of Grand-father clocks (to give them their Victorian name) have been made. The few early examples by such makers as Tompion are, of course, worth a great deal of money, but by far the greatest number of these clocks were made during a period of less than three quarters of a century, that is, from 1780 until 1850, by which date production had virtually ceased.

The best of grandfather clocks represent the pinnacle of both cabinet makers' and clockmakers' art, and good examples from the last half of the eighteenth century, with brass face and works and inlaid case in mahogany or walnut, can still be bought from £200 to about £400. However, for every brass-faced clock made, at least a hundred were produced with a painted iron face instead of the much more expensive and much more fashionable brass.

Many painted face clocks, particularly those of the eighteenth century, are in every other respect identical in design and quality to their brass-faced counterparts. But so great were their numbers that they have in the past been grossly undervalued, although prices have risen from around fifty shillings to more than as many pounds in the last few years.

Here, then, is the significant price gap into which a few of the wide boys in the trade have stepped. The equation is a simple one and could be described thus:

'One painted face clock, cost £80 plus legitimate profit of £10, equals £90. Subtract painted face and add brass at approximate cost of £15, equals clock now for sale at £300, giving a profit of £195 in all.'

The actual faking presents few difficulties, as the original painted face can be used as a template for size and shape, and a form is then

Grandfather or longcase clock, made by John Dalgleish of Edinburgh c. 1775.

cut from sheet brass. This is then engraved with suitable ornament, and often (quite illegally) with an actual clockmaker's name and town of supposed manufacture. No special tools are required, as the whole job can be given to an engraver.

The next part would be rather more difficult if it were not, again, for the ready services provided by specialist firms.

Some brass-faced clocks were made with a face cut and engraved from a single sheet of brass. Practically all the better examples, however, consist of the basic engraved plate, on to which are affixed the spandrels, the chapter ring, and usually the maker's nameplate. The chapter ring is the heavy brass or silvered brass ring on to which the hours or the 'chapters' are engraved, and the spandrels are the ornamental corner pieces of cast brass attached to the face.

Here again, perfectly respectable ornamental brassfounders advertise their services in the various antique and trade journals, and all one need do is order from their catalogues, which list all the necessary 'period' pieces together with any other embellishments, such as eagles and pillar finials, to enable the faker to make a really convincing job.

The finished fakes are good, so good in fact that more than one honest dealer has been fooled into buying examples through the trade.

I myself was offered no fewer than five recently, and since the price was reasonable, my first impulse was to buy, but a closer look revealed several faults.

The sheet brass used is hard and shiny and there are traces of machine buffing if the surface is looked at in an oblique light. The engraving does not quite fit the position of the spandrels or the chapter ring, and these parts are hard and new-looking, even if beautifully made.

However, it is at the back of the face that the presence of fakery is most revealing. Remove the hood of a genuine old brass-faced clock and, even if the works have been recently cleaned, the unmistakeable traces of hand-working, hammer and rivet marks, trial gravure marks, often even the craftman's name, are evident. All of this is missing on fakes, and all one sees is a blank sheet of hard and shiny modern looking brass.

I speak, of course, only of the fakes I have seen. Comparison of the genuine with the spurious readily shows the latter for what it is, but I appreciate that better and more difficult fakes could be made. The cost, however, would be much greater, and as the faker is only in the game for a quick and inflated profit, more time spent on accurate hand work and artificial 'ageing' means less profit, and to little point when there is such a ready market in any event.

One of the busiest fakers I know of has his 'factory' not far from

Edinburgh and, apart from judicious 'salting' in the trade, regularly sends his products to reputable auction rooms beyond his area of operations.

A longcase clock is a wonderful thing to have in the home. It is truly a thing of quiet joy and contentment to live with over the years and it is certainly still one of the best value for money buys available in antiques. But watch it!

Before buying, check all the points I have described and, finally, be sure to get a properly-worded guarantee of authenticity with your purchase.

11　Buying Silver

As the leaves fall from the trees and the tourists depart, then is the time for the overseas antique buyers to come to Britain, and the antique trade settles down to begin the serious business of the year.

Few tourists, from the New World at any rate, buy antiques. The North American market, in relation to the richness of the area and the population involved, is a poor one. Of course, most tourists from there will go back with some knick-knack or other and if it is a few years old, that is all the better. A small proportion, however, are serious and often knowledgeable collectors who happen to be tourists also and they will go home the richer, even if their purchases have been modest.

A higher proportion of Europeans will go back with at least one serious purchase, the Dutch and Germans with clocks and watches, the French with mother-of-pearl work, and the Italians, these Italians who seem endowed by nature with artists' eyes, will have bought everything which was 'carina' and which they were able successfully to haggle over.

Scottish Silver

How many people, however, tourist or native, realize that for as little as a couple of pounds they can buy a souvenir of Scotland which is both useful and made of solid silver. As a bonus, each customer will receive a picture of Edinburgh Castle and a Scottish thistle or the lion rampant badge of Scotland, together with the arms of the city of Glasgow and a miniature portrait of a past British monarch.

I refer, of course, to Scottish antique silver articles of the late eighteenth and early nineteenth century, which are both plentiful and cheap: cheaper, in many cases, than their modern equivalents. I exclude from this category early examples and important pieces, and also Scottish provincial silver, all of which is justifiably expensive.

However, a great deal of excellent silver was fashioned at both Edinburgh and Glasgow, mainly to furnish the tables of the new middle class that emerged after the union with England. It is no small tribute to the quality of the workmanship involved that the greater part of this silver seems to have survived, despite continual use, until the present day.

Apart from its distinctive and attractive marks, even the humblest of Scottish silver from this period is very beautiful. The Scottish silversmith had a love and respect for the metal which is reminiscent of the reverence of the early Chinese potter for his clay. This resulted in a simplicity of design, a grace combined with strength, which is difficult to define but at the same time is a most characteristic quality.

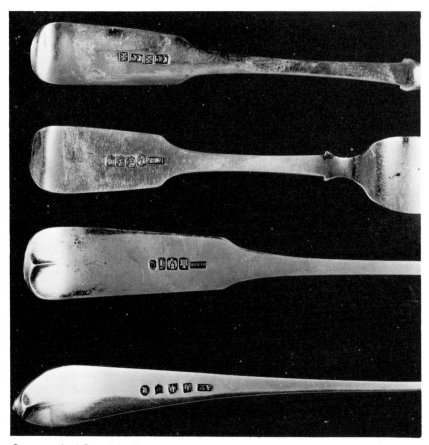

Some typical Scottish silver marks. From the top they are: Serving spoon, Alex. Ziegler, Edinburgh 1794; serving spoon, Robert Heron, Edinburgh 1814; fork marked W & S Glasgow, 1859; spoon, John Pringle, Perth, about 1820.

It is interesting and instructive to compare the recent history of antique Irish silver with Scottish silver of the same period. Five or six years ago, Irish silver—with the exception of rare provincial pieces —was extremely difficult to sell. Since then, despite the so-called slump in silver prices of 1969, it has become steadily rarer and dearer until the situation now is that Irish silver is difficult to find and there is a ready market even for pieces made in this century. It would appear

50

that the Irish have discovered their heritage in this respect at least, but the Scots seem sunk in their provincialism despite the treasure on their doorsteps.

The range of antique Scottish silver one can buy today is a very large one, even if a modest price limit of £30 is imposed. At this figure or a little below, there are the graceful and useful soup ladles of the late eighteenth century (nothing like these, combined with an old earthenware tureen, for making the canned variety taste better).

Later soup ladles tend to be heavier and to cost less, except for the types decorated with applied casting which I personally find less attractive. Hash or serving spoons range from about £15 to £20 and again the rules of age and pattern apply. For about £7 to £10 one can buy the smaller toddy or sauce ladles, and for a little less the tiny ladle-shaped condiment pieces which were often gilded inside the bowls, although this may have all but worn off.

Condiment spoons are as little as £1.50 and there are salt dishes to suit them. These are round or rectangular, and cost about £15 each. Sugar tongs, too, are another useful item; many people nowadays use them to dispense ice for drinks. These were made in a variety of patterns, plain, brightcut, 'Kings' pattern and so on, and a good George III pair should cost about £7.

Sets of small spoons—spoons were not made specifically for tea or coffee—if they are dated about 1790 will cost on the right side of £20. Georgian sets of larger spoons will cost a little above our £30 limit, as will the much scarcer forks which were uncommon in Scotland until about 1800. However, one can buy in multiples of two threes, three twos or a two and a four (just like the Irishman's change for a £6 note) and thus, by matching patterns, build up complete place settings for very little outlay.

Knives are rather a problem, as not so many silver-handled ones were made, and fewer still have survived. The old-fashioned bone or ivory-handled type is coming into favour, perhaps because of the quality of much of today's meat, and sets of these blend very well with silver, while their cost is very small indeed.

Cleaning Silver

There is a widespread belief that using silver articles involves a great deal of special polishing, but this is not so. Table silver which is used regularly should merely be washed in clean soapy water and dried with a dry cloth, and less-frequently used silver should be given a light rub about once a week with a soft duster. The use of special cleaners should be avoided, as these are abrasive and continual use is unwise.

If you are lucky enough to have some surplus capital, I can think of no more delightful way of putting it to sound long-term use than by buying one or two more important items of Scottish silver. If you think in terms of from £30 to about £200, the choice is a vast one, ranging from wine funnels through toast racks to fruit baskets.

Fine brightcut teapot by Alex Ziegler, Edinburgh 1785.

In my view about the nicest choice of all would be a teapot; either the late-eighteenth-century neo-classical shape, preferably with bright cutting, or the later or larger 'saddle' bellied kind standing on four ball feet. Silver prices are once more on their way up, but Scottish silver of the type and period I have described is no dearer than any other, a situation I am convinced will not long continue.

Meantime, I find it pleasant to think that our teapot which infuses such an excellent brew, was settling into middle age at the time of Waterloo and that Robert Burns could well have dined out using some of our cutlery.

12   The Romance of Porcelain

If the search for the Philosopher's Stone which would turn base metals into gold dominated the mind and energy of medieval man, then to an equally obsessive degree the search for the secret of porcelain making engrossed the kings and learned men of Europe for almost 150 years, throughout the seventeenth and much of the eighteenth century.

For over a thousand years, the Chinese had held their secret of making true porcelain: hard, non-porous, immensely strong and, above all, translucent. Early Europe had to content itself with crude stoneware, incapable of decoration in all but the most elementary sense, and totally unsuited for such flat surfaces as plates.

True, from the Moslem countries of the East came a technique of using a tin glaze on top of earthenware. This ware was, of course, quite opaque as was the glaze used with it, which had the advantage of covering up the rather unattractive colour of the body—and the disadvantage that any decoration had to be painted on to the surface of the glaze and fired at fairly low temperatures.

In the Arab-occupied countries of Spain, Southern Italy and Southern France, this tin-glazed earthenware began to be manufactured, and was variously called Majolica, Faience, and eventually in Holland, whence it spread from Spain, Delft.

Faience

Some wonderful ceramics have been produced in what I will now call Faience. The Isnik pottery of Turkey, the Hispano-Moresque wares, the Faience of Strasbourg and Lyons, the glorious colours of Deruta and Urbino, and the homely Delft of Holland and Britain (for it was made in Ireland and in Scotland, too). Lovely as it could be, however, Faience was soft, it crazed and chipped and became porous and it was almost useless for holding hot liquids. Above all, it did not possess that elusive quality of translucency.

Chinese Porcelain

Europe's first acquaintance with porcelain certainly came via the East, through Turkey and the Venetian republic. Later on, at the end of the fifteenth century, Chinese junks were bringing porcelain to the Philippines, and from there it was shipped aboard the yearly treasure

Chinese porcelain jar, late eighteenth century—Chien Lung period.

galleon to the isthmus of Panama, where it was transhipped at the Atlantic side on its final journey to Spain.

The opening up of the tea trade direct with China by the English, Dutch and Portuguese really made Europe aware of porcelain, and this period marks a watershed, both for European ceramics and also for Chinese porcelain.

Any discussion on Chinese porcelain must include the wares of the early dynasties, Han and Sung. These productions are beyond the pocket of the collector of limited means, but it is necessary, in my view, to appreciate their common standards, which was a respect for and a love of the material—and not, as one so often finds in modern European porcelain, using it as a vehicle on which to paint and decorate every available surface.

Thus the wares of Han and of Sung rely for their qualities almost entirely on shape and colour, and it is not until the dynasty of Ming, stretching from the fourteenth to the middle of the seventeenth century, that pictorial decoration as we normally think of it makes its appearance. With the coming of the Ming emperors, we are into the age of pictorially-decorated porcelain. Initially, the decoration was in deep blue. This colour, derived from cobalt, could be fired at very high temperatures; it could be applied under the glaze, with the resultant practical and aesthetic advantages of appearance and wearing qualities.

As the Ch'ing dynasty progressed through K'ang Hsi and Chien Lung, covering a period from the mid-seventeenth to the end of the eighteenth century, so the colours of the palette multiplied. These new colours were enamels painted over the glaze, but since they were enamel, i.e. glass, they were hard wearing and brilliant. Of those based on black, green or yellow, and later on pink and sky blue, perhaps the best known is the family of pink or rose enamels (actually a dye imported from Europe) known as 'Famille Rose'.

Despite this increasing sophistication in the range of the artist's palette, the best of Chinese decoration retained a great deal of its early qualities. A sparing use of detail, great delicacy in colour, a sense of quietness and tranquility—this has remained true of the best of Chinese porcelain up to the present day.

The European Influence

With increasing European influence in China, however, taste did degenerate in a general sense. Decoration became fussy and colours gaudier, while at the same time a major industry arose which catered specifically for the European, and later the North American market, with porcelain decorated in what the Chinese imagined to be European taste.

Surprisingly, from this seeming debasement of standards, much enchanting ware appeared. The reservoir of sheer artistry in China was so great that although—particularly in the mid-nineteenth-century—the so-called 'Cantonese' patterns degenerated into what was perilously near rubbish, there was a vast amount of porcelain produced, from vases to figurines to bowls and tea pots, that is quite charming in form, colour and vitality.

Tureen lid, Chinese underglaze blue—mid eighteenth century.

Scotland is, in this respect, singularly fortunate. As a nation with an important maritime tradition, the Scots still have for sale a great choice of Chinese porcelain, often at surprisingly low prices. The collector with enthusiasm and little money will seldom be able to buy really early ware, but he will find a great deal of underglaze blue from the eighteenth and seventeenth century and even earlier.

Porcelain Marks

At this point, may I say a little on the subject of marks. Much Chinese porcelain is marked with dynasty, reign and place marks, and although

56

puzzling at first they are not difficult to read. However, without any intention to deceive, the Chinese, with their traditional ancestor veneration, very often marked their porcelain with the date and name of a past master; as always, then, one's only guide in dating a piece should be on judgment of form, style and colour, and substance, based on experience.

Chinese fish tank, decorated in polychrome enamels c. 1800—late Chien Lung.

One great help to the tyro is that modern Chinese porcelain—that is, anything made after about 1870—lacks the distinctive pitting and imperfections, due to impurities, mainly iron, in the body, which is a characteristic of all Eastern porcelain before the advent of Western chemistry.

Apart from under the glaze blue ware, the enthusiastic collector who really wishes to search will find quite a lot of high-quality polychrome wares—mainly, it is true, from the late Chien Lung period, though often marked as from K'ang Hsi, and while specimens are not cheap, they can be purchased in good order for between £30 and £100 or so.

Imperfect Pieces

Apart from this, it is still possible to buy at remarkably low prices damaged pieces of the highest quality. Famille Rose plates, for instance, usually mended with copper rivets, and dating back as far as K'ang Hsi, can often be purchased for under £10, and even large bowls and jars in this condition are ludicrously cheap. This also applies to export ware made specifically for Europe, and much of this is armorial ware, decorated to order with various coats of arms.

A word of warning here: the famous firm of Samson of Paris made a great deal of 'Chinese' ware in the export and armorial manner. It is good but easy to spot, as there are absolutely no impurities in the body. Lastly, though a great deal of poor quality was produced in the last century to meet the demands of a vast market, much also continued to be made to high standards, both in the archaic styles and in contemporary taste. In this category, prices can be very modest indeed.

13   Unlocking the Secret of Porcelain

Porcelain long exercised a fascination for European minds because of its unique qualities, chief of which was its translucency. The only other substance known to sixteenth-century Europe which was plastic, and at the same time translucent, was glass—so perhaps it was natural that for over 150 years attempts to imitate porcelain were based on mixing ordinary china clay with ground glass.

Soft Paste Porcelain

In the absence of any systematic chemistry, and of any means of chemical analysis, it was natural that the two substances whose properties were known, china clay for its plastic and refractory qualities, and glass because not merely was it translucent, but at high temperatures it also became plastic, should be used in combination. This mixture, employed with varying success and with minor additions and alterations, is what is now known as 'soft paste' porcelain, to distinguish it from the 'hard' or true variety.

Soft paste porcelain was made at various times and at various places in Europe: in Italy, in France, and above all in England, where its manufacture was wider and lasted longer than elsewhere. It became somewhat refined by the substitution of steatite (a sort of glassy rock) for ordinary glass, and the addition of burnt animal bones to the mixture, both of which had the effect of 'hardening' the finished product.

'Soft paste' porcelain was not, of course, really soft, but took its name from the 'softer' or lower temperature at which it was fired, i.e., 1000 degrees centigrade as opposed to true porcelain which needs a temperature half as high again for firing.

In reading books on porcelain, it is all too easy to be blinded by the undoubted science of the experts, and I am often approached by someone in near despair who, after studying books describing the various soft paste manufacturers, is left only with a feeling of utter bewilderment. These people have my sympathy, and I do not want to add to the general confusion, especially as important articles made of soft paste are just not available to the collector of modest means.

It is necessary, however, to know soft paste by observation, not merely as a guide to dating but because it is still perfectly possible to pick up delightful little articles such as saucers and even cream jugs in

English soft paste of the mid-eighteenth century. The first lesson is to buy a piece of porcelain, preferably broken, which you can do for a couple of pounds or so, to enable you to observe its characteristics.

Soft paste porcelain very often exhibits small round areas of added translucency known as 'moons', visible when held to the light. Such flaws as firecracks and warping are frequent, and the glaze will almost certainly tend to 'pool' in corners and at the base around the footrim.

Coalport Plate c. 1810.

By the same token, the glaze will tend to 'creep' away from the edges of the footrim, leaving these parts free of glaze and often stained.

The actual glaze used on soft paste was liable to wear rather badly and specimens subjected to a great deal of use, such as plates, will almost invariably show signs of scratching. Lastly, although I do not recommend it, especially on a dealer's premises, a small file drawn across the footrim of a piece will cut into the body quite easily, while on true porcelain the file will make no impression.

There is, however, no substitute for handling as a means of learning; the broken edge of hard paste shows a fracture just like glass, while on soft paste the break will show first the layer of glaze, and then the granular body which resembles a layer of castor sugar.

Meissen figure: 'Taste', one of a group 'The Senses' c. 1840.

True Porcelain

While France and Italy were engaged on their experiments with soft paste formula, in the German principality of Saxony, at Dresden, things were moving on a rather different tack. Financed by the Saxon court, a nobleman by the name of Tschirnhausen, assisted by a rather dubious character called John Böttger, finally discovered the secret of making true porcelain. Surprisingly, the constituents were simple enough: china clay or kaolin, and a fusible feldespathic rock called petuntse. This mixture was fired at the very high temperature of 1500 degrees centigrade, and basically that was all there was to it.

What to Collect

Before going on to the practical aspect of porcelain collecting, I must say something about makers' marks. The 'crossed swords' mark of Meissen, with all its variants, is perhaps the best known and the most frequently copied mark in history. English factories and many on the Continent used it, and still continue to do so.

In short, a great deal of early porcelain is unmarked, particularly from such factories as Bow, and the only way to identify it with any degree of certainty is by a knowledge of style and period, and of the materials used in its manufacture. Any other approach is mechanical and dead, and far from leading to knowledge can bring only frustration.

What, then, to collect? Quite obviously there is little one can hope for in the way of early figures, especially from the Continent. A good Capo di Monte or Meissen group would buy a Rolls-Royce for both me and the wife, and still leave a couple of thousand over for incidentals.

It is, however, quite possible to spend a modest few pounds on a Meissen plate of the Marcolini period, or a Sèvres saucer or coffee can. I have even seen a Naples sucrier recently, made about 1770, with slight damage, but made in the very best baroque style, selling for £12.

In English ware, there are all sorts of small items both in hard paste and soft, such as cream jugs and coffee cans; the bargains, particularly in this field, are there for the knowledgeable buyer. If you are prepared to accept damaged pieces, and only a compound of a fool or a snob should not be, it is truly amazing what can still be purchased.

In this last respect, however, you will have to hurry; a glance at the illustrations in some of the recently published books on porcelain, or a visit to one of the better quality antique fairs, will show the extent to which damaged articles of quality are now being prized.

This word 'quality' is the linchpin of any sort of collecting. Porcelain after about 1835 has simply lost its craftsmanship and its style. Better always an article of quality, even if it has some damage, than a piece which is over-decorated and thoroughly bastard in its conception.

Some porcelain, particularly of the mid-nineteenth century, is a straightforward copy of earlier styles, and this is worth collecting for what it is; but in every other respect the above advice holds true.

14   Golden Age of Earthenware

Throughout the eighteenth century, despite the increasing flow of porcelain from China and the new porcelain factories springing up all over Europe, the traditional potters in earthenware went their own way. Porcelain, whether imported from the Orient or locally made, remained very much a luxury article, available only to the rich.

However, a new and numerous middle class was emerging, particularly in Britain, and if they could not afford porcelain they demanded at least much more refined designs in the traditional earthenware.

Faience

It was the first half of the eighteenth century which marked the golden age of the tin-glazed Faience we now call Delft, not only in the Dutch town of that name, but throughout France, England, and to an extent Scotland and Ireland also.

I have mentioned that the character of Faience embodied both its assets and its defects. The opaque glaze used covered up the unattractive clay, but soon chipped and crazed, as it was itself soft. But tin-glazed earthenware has great charm, and it has the vitality which all unsophisticated art forms seem to possess.

No Faience is cheap, and even damaged pieces, especially if they are unusual and have polychrome decoration, fetch good money; this, of course, merely bears out my oft-repeated advice to buy quality rather than condition. I have a soft spot for Faience collectors; the ware they collect is utterly charming and certainly one of the most satisfying things to collect.

Stoneware

In England, a type of earthenware called stoneware had long been made. This was manufactured from crushed flintstone and fired at a much higher temperature than ordinary earthenware. Stoneware was largely utilitarian, being used for flasks and bottles and mugs.

Its great density made stoneware non-porous and gradually, through the influence of such potters as John Dwight of Fulham, and due to such refinements in technique as burning the flintstone and using a glaze compounded of salt thrown into the kiln at a critical

64

temperature, the appearance of the ware was made much more attractive than the original dirty brown.

Creamware

Just about this time, in the 1740s, it was discovered that Devonshire, and to a lesser extent Dorset, had large deposits of fine white china clay and flintstone, and from these two items earthenware could be

Jugs, all last quarter of eighteenth century. Cream earthenware, Gordon's Factory, Prestonpans, Scotland.

produced of a fine creamy colour. For the first time, a transparent glaze, based on lead, could be used.

Hard on the heels of this discovery came yet another—the application of printed decoration to ceramics by means of transfer from an inked metal plate. As with so many important inventions, it would appear that several people were working on the idea at about the same time, but it seems that the firm of Saddler & Green in Liverpool were one of the first to employ the technique successfully.

During this time of expansion, change and innovation, a certain Josiah Wedgwood was serving as an apprentice in his brother's pottery at Burslem. We know little of Wedgwood's early life, but we do know that as a young journeyman he went into partnership with Thomas Wheildon for a period of five years, and this experience of working with one of Stafford's most competent potters must have been of immense value to him.

Wheildon was a master at decorating his ware with fine oxide glazes. These glazes, although they could not be painted on to give designs in the modern way, were very rich in tone and could be fired at very high temperatures, giving a most pleasing effect.

Scottish figures c. 1800. Jug, Watson's Pottery, Prestonpans c. 1820.

The art of figure moulding had just been introduced from France and proved very effective with the new improved stoneware bodies. It is almost certain that it was during this period that Wedgwood laid the foundation of his mastery of stoneware-making, which was to result in his famous Jasper ware.

Initially, however, it was the possibilities opened up by the new cream-coloured earthenwares which took most of Wedgwood's attention.

There were, of course, many fine potters working at this period: Wheildon, the Woods, Spode and many more who remain anonymous as they did not mark their wares in any way. Although the main centre of pottery-making was always in Staffordshire, there were important areas round Leeds and Liverpool, the Bristol Channel, and in Scotland, mainly in the Forth basin; all produced ware of the very finest quality, each with its distinctive characteristics.

66

Wedgwood apart, perhaps the most excellent of all this eighteenth-century earthenware was that produced at Leeds. Of astonishing lightness and delicacy, sparingly decorated or even quite plain, and with beautiful mouldings in both handles and finials, it is perhaps the loveliest earthenware produced anywhere at any time.

It must be conceded, though, that it is Wedgwood, with his versatility, his technical excellence, and his scorn for patent laws, who has left his mark most indelibly on the history of earthenware.

'The Sailor's Farewell': Jug from Prestonpans c. 1790.

Constant improvement in the body of his creamware, particularly by the addition of cobalt to improve its optical whiteness, resulted in the order for a huge dinner service for the Empress of Russia. In 1781 Wedgwood led the opposition to the renewal of the patent monopoly held by Champion for the exclusive use of Cornish clay and flint, and although Champion was allowed to keep his rights for the making of porcelain, from then on anyone could use the Cornish deposits in the manufacture of earthenware.

The year 1781 marks the turning point for British earthenware. Now socially accepted, of superlatively high quality, and with the raw materials of clay, stone and coal available to all, it was only a few years before it dominated the world's markets and, in the process, destroyed the traditional Faience industries of the Continent.

What to Collect

As to the opportunities available to the collector in search of early earthenware today, I will try to summarize these as briefly as possible, although the field is a vast one. No one should ignore the possibility, which still does arise, of picking up small articles of Faience, particularly Delftware. Usually these will be Dutch and very often tiles; the latter are particularly desirable, for apart from being attractive in themselves, they represent the opportunity to examine a cross-section of the body.

Remarkably, it is not difficult to buy at modest prices seventeenth- and eighteenth-century examples of brown stoneware, usually in jugs or mugs. Of course a great deal has been copied by such firms as Doulton, but a handy test is to examine the embossed decoration which most of these articles carry. The reproduction stoneware is moulded, body and decoration, in one piece, while the genuine article has the decoration 'sprigged' on to the body from small plaster moulds, which show distinct joins, often allowing the corner of a fingernail to be inserted.

The Jasper ware of Wedgwood is well known and usually marked, but in any case American demand and that market's obsession for marked ware has sent prices to impossible heights. This is true also of the rather similar black Basalte ware, but it is often forgotten that a great many firms made Jasper and Basalte wares—Turner of Lane End, Spode, Ridgeway and Hilditch. It was even made in Prestonpans.

Such firms as Spode, Riley and Rogers and many more made blue and white printed ware of a very high standard indeed. The shades of blue in this earlier printed pottery are of a very subtle nature; the printing is crisp and precise, the subjects legion, and the potting is so 'tight' that one can often feel it 'sing' in the hand.

With the exception of the early-nineteenth-century invention of the hybrid 'ironstone' body, all earthenware made between the second half of the eighteenth century and about 1820 is remarkably light in weight, and the standard of potting is often higher than that of porcelain of the same period.

Decoration is invariably charming, and while many pieces are decorated in Chinoiserie, others bear designs to satisfy the taste of a highly localized market, so that one comes across themes of farming, shipwreck and seafaring, and all sorts of trades from collier to farrier, as well as political events recording such themes as the Peterloo Massacre or the threat of French invasion.

Figures and groups were also made extensively, and it is a mistake to think of these as some sort of poor relation of the same thing in porcelain. Earthenware figures were being made in Stafford long before Chelsea, and while many of the English porcelain figures are rather insipid copies of Meissen, the earthenware variety are entirely native to Britain. Both modelling and decoration are vigorous and appealing, and the actual models are often based on local characters.

68

Scottish pottery can claim importance in this respect and the figures from Rathbone's pottery in Portobello of fisherfolk and street musicians are typical examples. None of these early figures is cheap if in good order, but the £55 or so you will have to pay is a much better buy than either the porcelain equivalent or the later Victorian 'named' flat-back rubbish.

15 Sheffield Plate: Marriage of Copper and Silver

In the year 1743, two years before Charles Edward Stuart finally took the plunge and landed at Moidart, a certain metal worker from Sheffield, who rejoiced in the name of Thomas Balsover, made a most important discovery. Silver and copper, he noted, had exactly the same ductile qualities; that is, subjected to pressure by either beating or rolling, silver and copper will stretch to exactly the same degree and in exactly the same manner.

By making up an ingot consisting of a 'sandwich', with its centre of copper and its outer of thinner layers of silver, it was possible, Balsover demonstrated, to roll out a sheet of what appeared to be pure silver, at a fraction of the cost of the real thing. This substitute material was known as Sheffield Plate.

To understand the importance of this discovery, it is necessary to appreciate two things. First, in the eighteenth century silver was, in real money terms, a much more precious metal than it now is. The price of bullion silver was something like five times its present day level, but at the same time highly skilled craftsmen were plentiful and by no means well paid.

The other factor we must bear in mind is that there was, until Balsover's discovery, absolutely no other substitute for silver in existence. We who live in a world where electroplate, steel made stainless, and chromium are commonplace, must try to think back to a world where there was either silver for those who could afford to enjoy both its practical and aesthetic advantages, or the only alternatives—pewter, soft, short-lived and still fairly expensive, quite apart from its toxic nature, or steel, which tainted food and required constant scouring.

By the 1760s, Sheffield Plate was already well established, and used for a wide variety of articles, from sword mounts to candlesticks, apart from its more obvious uses at the table, when that early apostle of mass production, Matthew Boulton, came upon the scene. Boulton was a Birmingham silversmith who had the courage and the imagination to make a long list of parts for silver articles; such things as legs for teapots and salvers, knops for lids, silver hinges and ornamental swags. His products were both cast and hammered (the latter by ingenious foot-operated drop forges), and the silversmith had only to order ex-catalogue from Boulton's pattern book.

Soon he was producing similar items in Sheffield Plate, but in this

Sheffield Plate hot water container c. 1790.

case hammered only as, of course, it was not possible to cast in the new material. This, the combination of the inventive genius of both Balsover and Boulton, is the Sheffield Plate which is sought after by collectors today.

I did say 'sought after' but I will also add that it is not sought after enough, and that there is still a great deal of silly snobbery attached to its collection. The reason for this snobbery lies in the fact that since the layer of silver on Sheffield Plate is very thin, the copper eventually shines through, particularly in those areas subject to most wear. A piece thus worn is described as 'bled' and, until recently at least, no matter how attractive it was in appearance it would not be considered collectable.

'Why', you may ask, 'cannot a worn piece be replated?' The answer is that it can and often is, and the result is disastrous, for Sheffield Plate is a mechanical process and electroplating is a chemical method of coating, which is quite unsuitable to this material. We all grow old, people and things, but the test of real beauty is that it grows old gracefully and has no need of facelifting, like some superannuated harlot.

Sheffield Plate was made by craftsmen; by exactly those same craftsmen who made articles of hallmarked silver and in exactly the same way, i.e. by hand beating, rolling and shearing. Copper in its way is just as lovely as silver, while the visible combination of the two, as in 'bled' Sheffield Plate, can be superb.

Sheffield Plate, except from a few specialist dealers, is not expensive to buy. In 'bled' condition, its price is usually quite modest, that is to say it should cost less than modern silver plate from a department store, and it is not merely attractive to look at but it is extremely functional in the home, in such items as wine slides, condiment sets, trays, tea caddies, candlesticks, tea and coffee pots and a whole host of others. Like every exercise in recognition, it requires more than reading about it to attain proficiency and again, my advice is to go to a reputable dealer who will be very willing to show you items both in electroplate and Sheffield Plate, let you handle both, and point out how they differ.

The first thing you should notice is the beautiful soft glow which Sheffield has, in comparison with the hard and 'dead' appearance of the electroplated article, no matter how bright it may be. This is because the hand beating in Sheffield Plate imparted a glow as in old silver, made even lovelier by the added glow from the underlying copper. While, as I have already mentioned, there will probably be copper exposed on these areas subject to most wear, some edges and banding may show no signs of wear, and in this event they have been protected by pure silver wire or sometimes by Boulton's cast silver mounts.

72

Sheffield Plate cruet set—the bottles have silver tops hallmarked for 1803.

This is particularly so when it has become necessary to conceal the tell-tale sheared edge, which of course would reveal the copper core of the material. Sheffield Plate could not be engraved, although it was sometimes what is known as 'flat hammered' to simulate engraving, and I have seen presentation pieces with a lozenge of silver let in, so that an inscription could be engraved thereon. One will also see such articles as salvers and wine slides with cast pewter ornaments, which have been tinned over, and condiment sets with hallmarked silver-topped bottles while mounted on a Sheffield Plate holder.

Much Sheffield Plate was marked, often with maker's punch marks only, but late in the eighteenth century many pieces were marked with punches which came dangerously close to the correct hallmarks of the period. However, as this practice eventually harmed the reputation of the silversmiths themselves, all marking was eventually forbidden.

Finally, as Sheffield Plate making died out in the 1830s, everything that was made was in good taste and in the classical manner. Indeed, the limitations imposed by the material imparted a discipline to the craft, even greater at times than that of the silversmith proper, so that the best of Sheffield Plate is akin to Scottish silver in its clarity and simplicity of form.

16 Beware those Bargains in Pewter

Recently I received a request from the trustees of a museum in the United States for suitable pieces of pewter which they wanted rather urgently. The story of this particular museum is quite fascinating in itself, and shows just what can be done if sufficient intelligent and concerned people get together, talk a bit, agree on a plan of action, and then act on it.

Briefly, a group of citizens in New York were aware that in their area lay the remains of a village which had been a pioneer community in the middle and late eighteenth century. So they got together and decided to rebuild and furnish the village as it once was.

With American efficiency, they formed a limited company in order to raise the necessary capital for the project. Progress has been so satisfactory that there is no reason to suppose that eventually it will not be a success from both an educational and a financial standpoint.

At the moment, they are working on the village inn, and the request for suitable pewter arose from this. Very sensibly, the committee decided that while insisting on authenticity and pieces from the correct period, they do not demand that everything be in pristine condition. They reasoned, quite correctly, that many articles must have been used in a damaged and mended condition.

This commonsense attitude has, in the past, made it much easier for me to supply specimens of early earthenware at reasonable prices.

Early pewter is, of course, both scarce and dear and when the request from my friends came along I did not have much in stock; so I set off to see what I could find.

It never ceases to surprise me what still turns up in Britain when one really looks. At almost my first call, I bought a lovely Queen Anne coffee pot, in pewter, for under ten pounds. True, the original handle had been lost some time before and replaced with one of brass, but it was an old replacement and the pot had survived almost 300 years of use with this sole damage.

My next call, farther north, yielded a surprise of rather a different nature, for here I was offered, in rather a posh establishment, a pewter 'tappit hen' for £42. Under normal circumstances, of course, this price for such a desirable piece would be a real bargain, but this particular 'hen' was, so to speak, fresh off the nest—and carried, of all things, a LONDON touch mark. London marks, indeed, on an article never made outside of Scotland.

Of all antiques, pewter is perhaps the most consistently faked and reproduced, and while most copies like this tappit hen are easy to spot, this is not always the case. One of the first problems facing the tyro collector is to define what exactly pewter is. To emphasize this difficulty, I have just finished reading an otherwise excellent book on pewter, which does not once mention what the metal consists of!

Genuine pewterware: Left, Scots tappit hen 'stoup' c. 1760 (from Mr Colin Stead's collection); centre, Scottish imperial pint measure (from same collection); rear, plate by London maker c. 1780; right, Queen Anne coffee pot with replacement handle (see text).

Basically, pewter is an ally comprising about 80 parts tin to 10 parts copper and the same of lead. Sometimes, a little antimony may have been added to the mixture, and the proportions were never in any case constant, chiefly because a great deal of 'wrythen'—metal from melted down old pieces—was used.

Strict control of quality, however, both of the metal and of workmanship, was effected by the guilds and incorporations of pewterers (in Scotland, the incorporations of Hammermen); the system of marks or 'touches' used by these guilds provide the collector today with much fascinating information.

Each master pewterer had to punch his touch on a master plate kept by his guild, and thereafter he was compelled to use this touch and no other on the items he made. The original touchplate of the Edinburgh Incorporation of Hammermen is extant, and can still be seen in the National Museum of Antiquities.

Pewter at one time was used in the making of a variety of articles— ranging from buttons to church chalices. It is a comparatively soft metal, however, and vessels made from it generally were not expected to last. There was, indeed, an established trade-in system operating. The pewterer would give his customers an allowance on their old vessels in part exchange for new, which is one reason why early specimens are rare.

Some early pewter, too, has grown a hard oxide 'skin' through neglect, and collectors often can't agree on what treatment, if any, should be given. Pewter was made to sustain a high polish; if it has been properly kept, it will appear shining, but darker than old silver. If oxidization is very advanced, however, I prefer to polish the article with wax and leave it at that.

Shapes in pewter follow closely the styles in silver of the same period and this, apart from touch marks, is a very valuable aid to full identification. Scotland has a special place in the affections of pewter collectors, as there is a complete range not only of Scottish vessels, but of Scottish measures, to go with them. Before the year 1826, the pint Scots called the 'Stoup' was almost equal to three pints imperial measure. There were correspondingly smaller measures such as the 'Chopin' and the 'Mutchkin' to accommodate the not-so-drouthy.

These and their brethren were produced in various sizes of the famous 'hen', with or without its 'tap', and sometimes in a range of lidded, baluster-shaped tankards favoured particularly in the west. Also used—though it earned an infamous reputation—was a range of spirit measures in the shape of a thistle. This particular thistle was eventually banned, as it was easily 'emptied' in such a way as to leave the landlord's share still in the bottom.

Ireland, too, had its own particular types of measure, notably the lovely 'haystack', so named for its resemblance in shape to the stacks in the Irish fields.

By the late eighteenth century, pewter was already on the way out although its use, mainly in pubs, continued until well into the Victorian era. The competition from strong white earthenware on the one hand, and from such new materials as Britannia metal, proved to be overwhelming. Britannia metal, an alloy of antimony and tin which could be produced on factory lines by spinning on a lathe, was much cheaper to make than the traditional pewterer's method of casting and hammering.

Britannia metal is often sold today as pewter—and at pewter

prices, often by those who should know better. Apart from this fiddle, there are various gentry turning out all sorts of fake pewter articles, complete with the touch marks of the supposed period.

Unfortunately, there is nothing in law which prevents the marking of reproduction pieces in this way, and in any event, many genuine old pieces escaped marking at the time they were made. Fortunately, few of these modern fakes, made as they are with inferior metal and produced on the lathe, would deceive any reasonably intelligent person. Pewter, however, has been faked for a very long time, and many of these productions of 50 years or so ago, in addition to being well made, now carry a little genuine patina of age.

The moral, of course, when spending more than a few pounds, is always to go to a dealer on whose honesty and expertise you can rely. By all means look for bargains, but never spend much on them or you may find that your bargain has been an expensive mistake.

17   The Magic of Eastern Carpets

One of the nice things about dealing in antiques is the opportunity to learn about fresh items in which to deal. As some classes of goods become so rare as to preclude the non-specialist from handling them, another avenue opens up, as one's interests, commercial and aesthetic, are forced to turn elsewhere.

As they say philosophically in my native Ireland: 'Shure when one door closes, another one shuts.' So it is that I have become seriously interested in Eastern or, as common parlance has it, 'Persian' carpets and rugs.

'Persian' is a name given to all the rugs woven by hand in all the areas of the Near and Far East, and which are traditional amongst Moslem peoples. To my mind, they are one of the best buys in near-antiques today. These rugs are attractive in appearance, complement any furnishing scheme, and except for very fine specimens, are surprisingly cheap to buy—often cheaper than their machine-made copies.

I have no wish, in this limited space, to trot out a whole string of names and data, such as Baluchi, Kirgitz or Tabriz. This would be quite pointless for the average person wishing to pick up a cheery rug for the hall or the fireside. There are, however, a few commonsense pointers to keep in mind when purchasing Eastern rugs, and these I propose to outline.

Knots per Square Inch

The first and most important factor is the number of knots used to the square inch, which invariably determines the quality of the rug. Fairly good rugs start about 80 knots to the inch and, as quality increases, can go up to well over the 250 mark, which is, when you think of it, a very great deal indeed. Obviously, the more knots the better the wearing qualities, but in addition to this the number of knots used in a given area governs the complexity of colours and patterns which can be obtained.

At the lower end of this scale, one finds the typical Indian rug with a long loose pile, and very little in the way of wearing qualities, and having, of course, a rough pattern only. Next we have the coarse but much harder-wearing Turkish rug, with about 25 knots to the square inch; a little up the scale, Chinese and Baluchi rugs both have about

50; rugs from the Caucasus can have up to 100 knots to the square inch, while Bokhara and Kashan types can very from 200 to 280 or thereabouts.

Designs in rugs are traditional, and with the exception of some truly Persian patterns—and in obedience to the Koran—are based on geometric forms, rather than pictures of living things. Many were made as prayer rugs, and as such have the 'mihrab' or representation of the mosque door worked into the pattern.

There is one variety of rug which is very satisfactory in use, although the pattern is seldom of much interest, and that is the typically long-piled and tough 'Turkish' rug from Anatolia.

Condition

Condition is the next point for inspection, and in this context one must remember two things: first, the amount of wear acceptable on an Eastern carpet or rug is much greater than one would accept on the European article—a worn rug can still be quite serviceable and visually pleasing; second, in nomad-made rugs, defects in size, uneven finishing at the ends, and inconsistency of colour shades have nothing to do with quality, but merely reflects the particular conditions under which the rug was made.

Design and Colour

This brings me to my last factor in judging quality, which is design and colour. As a general rule, the older the rug, the less likely it is that colours based on aniline dyes will have been used. Colours obtained from these dyes are harsh, particularly when new, and tend to fade quickly and to 'run' more readily than colours obtained from vegetable dyes; it must be emphasized, of course, that a certain degree of fading is inevitable with any rug.

The design, too, is not to be condemned if it is rather basic and confined to only a very few colours. This is because while a coarse weave obviously limits the complexity of the pattern, very many high quality rugs have been confined to a simple colour scheme and pattern, through deliberate choice on the part of the weaver.

Personally, I always like to look at the back of a carpet or rug first, and I think you obtain a better idea of its basic qualities in this way, without being distracted by other and subsidiary factors.

I was discussing trade in general recently with an old country dealer, and we got round to the subject of eastern carpets. He told me a tale—or it may be a parable—and I would like to relate it here.

It seems that the dealer's father, some 40 years before, headed a little syndicate, which did very well selling odd surplus items from

A typical nomad rug from Afghanistan.

country mansions to certain well-heeled clients, particularly in the United States. Word went round the trade that a certain gentleman, well known in the operatic world, was interested in acquiring a Persian carpet of the very best quality.

The little group, consisting of seven members, held a meeting and agreed on a plan of action. There was cash available, but unfortunately no one knew of a carpet with a suitable pedigree available for immediate sale, so it was decided that the mountain, so to speak, would have to go to Mahomet. Accordingly, seven railway tickets were purchased to Istanbul—or, as my friend pronounced it, 'Istantbul'.

Arriving safely in Turkey, the syndicate bought a carpet of quality for around £1000 and set off home again for Scotland. At Paris, however, a difference arose over some points of investment, and as is usual among dealers in such cases a 'knock-out' was held, which resulted in four members being bought out of the group.

The three remaining travellers then entered their carpet for sale in the forthcoming auction of a famous London firm, and sent the 'inside information' to their prospective client that a carpet of just the quality he wanted was due to come on the London market before long.

Came the day of the sale, and our syndicate attended as keen bidders for what was undoubtedly a very fine lot. They threw the ball to each other during the bidding, and long after other interested parties had dropped out, they kept on, until they had the carpet knocked out, to themselves of course, for £4000.

Our friends now had a carpet, with a cast iron provenance, and the hard valuation of open bidding at a famous auction house to back its undoubtedly deserved claim to excellence. The theatrical gentleman (since departed this earth) agreed to purchase it for £5000—a sum which, 40 years ago, showed quite a tidy profit indeed. Everyone concerned—owners, auction firm, and purchaser—was happy.

18　The Story of a Punch Bowl

Most of the antique dealer's week is spent in handling what I might call 'predictable' things. Of course, to someone outside the trade a Grandfather clock, a mahogany bureau or a Georgian silver teapot all have a certain exotic quality. To the dealer, however, no matter how much he may appreciate his work, these items form the bread and butter (and at least some of the jam) of his business.

The real thrill is in coming across the unusual; the celadon plate among the odd lot, the silver spoons with a rare provincial mark, the seventeenth-century pocket sundial sold as an incomplete Victorian compass. Discoveries like these do not necessarily make one's fortune, for age and rarity are not always as highly regarded by a fickle public as they should be. It always gives me pleasure, however, when I buy something previously unrecognized for what it is, and at the same time turn a modest £10 into a somewhat less modest £35 or so.

This happy circumstance happened to me recently when I called at a small shop, half antique and half gift shop, at a seaside town in the north-east. It is always rather difficult for a trade buyer to find much in a shop of this nature, for naturally enough the sort of stock held reflects the kind of trade done, and I do not mean this observation to be derogatory in any way.

Among the Victorian Stafford figures and assorted brass, however, was one item that almost made my heart miss a beat: a most lovely, although damaged, Chinese export ware porcelain bowl. Not merely was this bowl a particularly fine example of Chinese porcelain made in the eighteenth century for the European market, but it had been made specially for a masonic lodge. It was, in fact, a 'one off' piece and had in all probability been ordered as a punch bowl for a local lodge.

Most history books seem to give the impression that, for the average person at least, life in Europe before the Industrial Revolution— before, that is, mechanical forms of transport—was very much a system of isolated communities, existing without much contact with each other and still less with the outside world. I have formed the view from my own experience that this assumption needs to be radically modified, particularly where a community had the sea at its doorstep and as a part of its living.

The growth in the quantity of Chinese porcelain exported to Europe during the eighteenth century bears me out. Not only was porcelain exported from China—porcelain indistinguishable from that supplied to the home market—but an industry developed which made porcelain shaped and decorated to distinctively European requirements. The Chinese had no use for such things as tureens and sauceboats, coffee pots and cream jugs, but they were quick to copy European shapes and adapt to the needs of another civilization.

The Chinese idea of decoration, too, was not to European taste generally. Traditionally, the Chinese decorated their wares in a style that today would doubtless be described as 'cool'. They delighted in the harmony of form, shape and colour, and the best of Chinese work

Chinese export ware masonic punch bowl.

has the most wonderful sense of tranquility made effective by an absolute economy of form and brushwork.

The European, on the other hand, demanded decoration portraying the exotic East and plenty of it. He wanted as many figures and as much background in as many colours as possible, and so long as the whole effect gave him value for money, he was not really fussy if turbans were worn in China or pigtails in India. The Chinese, as always, were only too pleased to satisfy the market and the wares they exported to Europe in vast quantities are remarkably pleasing, although the Chinese themselves would not have given them house room.

Surprisingly, in view of the quantity made, it was generally assumed until well into the present century that most of this Chinese export ware was not Oriental at all but made at the English pottery at Lowestoft. Indeed, you can still find people in the antique business who speak of 'Chinese Lowestoft', assuming that the ware was at least decorated in England.

The small potworks at Lowestoft did in fact manufacture only soft paste porcelain, which is not a true porcelain but a substitute made during the eighteenth century in England and in France. It should be noted, however, that since certain items of domestic pottery had to be

Late-eighteenth-century Chinese export ware teapot. The handle has been replaced by a 'tinker's mend'.

taken to China for the Chinese to copy, and since some at least of these specimens would have been decorated in Chinoiserie, the Chinese not only copied the shapes but the decoration as well, so that we are left with a Chinese copy of an English picture of a 'Chinese' scene!

Another and quite distinct type of Chinese export porcelian is the specially commissioned piece. My bowl is in this category and it is a sobering thought that when it was made, about 1770, you could send the pattern required to Shanghai or Canton via one of the tea ships sailing the China run, and within a year it would be made and decorating the table of some lodge or friendly society or private home. All of which shows, to my mind at least, that the eighteenth-century world was not such a system of watertight compartments as some historians would have us believe.

Time came when most of the shipping offices and many of the ships'

Porcelain Plate with design of Scottish Highlanders: Chinese, eighteenth century. (Photograph by courtesy of The Royal Scottish Museum, Edinburgh.)

captains carried pattern books issued by the Chinese merchants. From these you could order all sorts of pieces, even complete dinner sets, and have them decorated with designs including crests and coats-of-arms. If you did not possess a crest, then the pattern book could be used to permutate any number of suitable and impressive initials, coats-of-arms and cartouches.

The Latin in the mottoes was often a bit shaky and, of course, when it came to painting a European face the Chinese could no more do this with success than a European could paint Chinese features. The end result of this artistic endeavour was often comical in the extreme. The faces painted on my masonic bowl, of the sun and the moon for instance, are distinctly non-European.

There exists in the Royal Scottish Museum, Edinburgh a plate depicting two very oriental-featured bagpipe players, fully kilted and accoutred in the authentic eighteenth-century manner. I have also seen a plate with a copy of a Hogarth cartoon depicting a kilted Scotsman. Since Hogarth hated all Scotsmen, the end result, which is a copy of a caricature, can be imagined.

There exists also a rare class of 'Christian' or 'Jesuit' Chinese export ware, and one piece I recollect has the most touching scene of Christ; a Chinese Christ on the cross of Calvary.

Large pieces of Chinese export ware, particularly the armorial variety, have always been in demand. Indeed, at the turn of this century much more was being paid in the saleroom for this class of porcelain than now.

The firm of Samson of Paris obligingly stepped in to ease the shortage and their copies, well made if a trifle florid, now fetch good money for what they are. These copies, however, are often sold as the genuine article, although they are not difficult to spot as they are made in European porcelain, which has none of the typical impurities in the body, so much a feature of the Chinese variety.

As in many other aspects of antique collecting, the British do not appreciate just how lucky we still are when it comes to buying Chinese porcelain made for export in the eighteenth century. Modest pieces can still be bought quite easily for a few pounds, and that amount can quite often become even less if the article is damaged.

My bowl cost me £5 and, had it been perfect, this rare piece could easily have fetched many hundreds. As things turned out, I sold it for £30. I am sure the seller made a profit both in money and in knowledge and the buyer, I know, does not grudge me my lucky strike. For my part I both made money and had lots of fun.

19   In Search of a Bargain

The tale has often been told of the North American Indian and his defeat, not by the guns or the whisky of the white man, but by the slaughter and final disappearance of the buffalo on which his life depended. Like the buffalo, certain classes of antiques which for years have given a comfortable living to some dealers both here and abroad have virtually gone from the market and will never return.

A friend said to me the other day: 'If you see a Dutchman with a glazed look wandering about the Grassmarket, don't worry. He is only an antique dealer looking for Grandfather clocks.' The Dutchman will, I am afraid, have to turn elsewhere for his living, like the Danish seamen I know who used to ship clocks regularly back to Denmark, often packing four at a time inside the ship's dummy funnel.

Not merely clocks are involved, of course. The list may end there but it starts at jelly pans (how many brass jelly pans were made in Scotland I wonder) and works its way right through miners' lamps and candlesticks, taking in Victorian furniture on the way.

The writing is, in other words, on the wall for the big shipping dealer who, despite his present progression from Victoriana to Edwardiana, cannot hope to obtain the vast quantities of goods necessary for his kind of trade.

For the small dealer, however, determined to maintain a reasonably good standard in the quality of goods he handles, the opportunities are still there and always will be. It does mean, though, that he has to work increasingly hard and spend more and more of his time out of the shop and on the road.

Another friend, an American, carried this technique of 'looking' to the heights of an art. He was a footloose character who made his living as a 'runner', that is, the kind of dealer who has no shop but merely buys and sells to other dealers.

His equipment consisted of a notebook, a torch, a camera and a pair of binoculars. Any item which interested him, but which he either could not buy or did not wish to risk money on, he would photograph and measure, entering the dimensions and other details in his book. His torch was for use when he came to a shop which was closed, and by methodical use of its light plus his binoculars, he could check pretty well every item on display.

My friend had both a card index and a card-index mind, and a great deal of his time was spent in whatever public library was handy,

Frontispiece from Kyssel's Iconographia.

checking details of his purchases, both actual and prospective, not least of these being the records of prices obtained at auction for similar items.

Every man to his own poison, of course. While I like to know what I am buying and selling, such methodical fanaticism seems rather extreme. But it can pay off, and I remember one occasion when my friend bought a Chinese brown and white decorated bottle in Perthshire. It was a pretty bottle, although rather badly chipped at the neck, and because of this the shopkeeper sold it for 30 shillings. A little research established that the bottle was from the Sung dynasty, was of the kind usually referred to as a 'pilgrim flask', and was in fact a very rare piece.

My friend sold it for £3000 and went back to America on the proceeds. I seldom go into the reference section of the library without this episode crossing my mind.

Recently in the library I started to look at one of the volumes of auction records which some of the major London-based auction firms publish yearly, and I noted that the 'Christie-Miller' table service of Meissen had changed hands two years previously at £68,000—or rather more than £1000 per piece.

In common, I am sure, with millions of others, I was unaware of this very early and most unusual Meissen service. It was unusual, the book

89

90

Pallazzo deß Ambasciator von Franckreich, zu Venedig in Canal Regio

Page from Kyssel's Iconographia, on which decoration of Christie–Miller Meissen service is based.

explained, because the decoration was based on a series of engravings of Italian, Spanish and German views by one Melchior Kussell, who also called himself Melchior Kysell, and published at Augsburg in 1682. Unfortunately, the book went on, the absence of a complete

Part of the Christie-Miller dinner service from the Meissen factory. The author believes he has the volume of prints on which the decoration of the porcelain is based. (Photograph by courtesy of Sotheby's.)

volume of the engravings made it at present impossible to identify each scene decorated on the porcelain.

Well, lament no longer, for I have what is probably a complete set of the engravings in my possession. I bought these some time ago for £30 and, because they were complete in one volume with four frontispieces, one for each section of the series, and because they were all original sharp impressions and dated, I thought I could afford to overlook the somewhat tatty state of some. Somehow or other I never really tried to sell the volume, I think because I hated the thought of some print dealer splitting it up.

The point of my story, of course, is that there will always be plenty of room for the small antique dealer provided he works hard and does his homework. Perhaps to emphasize my point, I had a call from the man who bought my Chinese masonic bowl which I sold for £30. He was delighted to show me a picture and a description of an identical but undamaged bowl which sold at auction recently for £1675. Like the good fellow that he is, my customer has promised to leave it to me in his will. Ah well, that's show business.

20 Armoury of the Clans

The Claymore

I suppose that in the antique business, especially in Scotland, there are few more evocative terms than the single word 'claymore'. At the same time, there can be few other objects, military or otherwise, which are so consistently mis-identified, and about which so much romantic nonsense has been written.

Every year, as the tourist season gets into full swing, in practically every antique shop in Scotland, you can be sure of a continuous stream of overseas visitors, all asking the same question: 'Have you got any claymores?'

What they are looking for, of course, is not the claymore, 'claidheamh mor' or 'big sword' in Gaelic, but its much later successor, the basket-hilted broadsword, most commonly associated with the Jacobite rebellion, and still worn, in a debased form, by officers of certain Scottish regiments.

Like the basket-hilted broadsword, the claymore was not really a Scottish weapon at all, although it is true that both weapons, through long use in Scotland, eventually acquired distinctively Scottish characteristics.

If one single thing characterized the nature of Scottish society, and particularly that of the Highlands up to the middle of the eighteenth century, it was its essential conservatism, and this was illustrated most pointedly by the retention of certain types of weapons, and of military techniques, long after they had been discarded by the rest of Europe.

An Italian chronicler of the fifteenth century, just after the time of the great English condottiere Sir John Hawkwood, describes the amusement of the Florentines at the sight of a band of Scottish mercenaries who had just entered the service of Florence. 'Their helmets and breastplates were of the most ancient kind, they marched to the sound of a rude bagpipe such as our shepherds play, and they carried such long swords slung on their backs, of a pattern which were once used on the crusades against the Turks.'

The true claymore, then, was really the two-handed sword common to most of Europe when swordplay consisted largely of bash and slash. In Scotland, this sword tended to be somewhat smaller, or 'hand and half' size, and developed the distinctive down-drooping quillons (the cross-pieces at the foot of the hilt) which one always associates with the claymore.

The Broadsword

The basket-hilted type of sword was a natural development of the decline in the use of armour, and consequently of the need to provide some protection for the once-gauntleted hand. Once more, however, though swords became smaller and developed into auxiliary thrusting weapons with the general use of musketry, combined with the pike and later the bayonet, the Scottish Highlander still clung to his traditional broadsword, in the belief that it was the weapon of a gentleman.

Thus the broadsword, like the claymore before it, became a distinctively Scottish weapon, and the baskets assumed differing forms, often of great beauty; from them we can identify the period in which they were made, and often the place and even the maker.

The blades, too, are fascinating. Many of them, particularly from the seventeenth and early eighteenth centuries, are marked 'Andrea Ferrara', and there has been much speculation about the origins of this name.

Although all sorts of judgments have been given as final, the verdict is really an open one, and blades so marked could have been made in Scotland by a family of immigrant Italians from Ferrara, just as the McCrimmons may well have been itinerant musicians from Cremona. Some blades bear the 'running wolf' mark of Solingen, as well as the Ferrara mark, and they could possibly have originated in Germany.

The Dirk and the Targe

The other main armament of the Highlander was a dirk or long-bladed knife, which he normally held with the left hand in much the same way as the classical 'main gauche' of the continent, although the Highland weapon lacked the long quillons which made the Continental one such a powerful parrying ally. The fighting dirk of the eighteenth century or earlier was, of course, a very different weapon from the knife and fork, jewel-studded variety, beloved of the Victorian age.

However, the lack of a weapon with which to parry and defend his left side forced the Highlander to retain his shield, or targe, made of brass-studded bull hide, for some two and a half centuries after the shield had been discarded in the rest of Europe.

Pistols

One weapon the Scottish clansman did add to his armoury in a very distinctive form was the pistol; but, even so, firearms were seldom used north of the Highland Line until the matchlock and wheel lock had

94

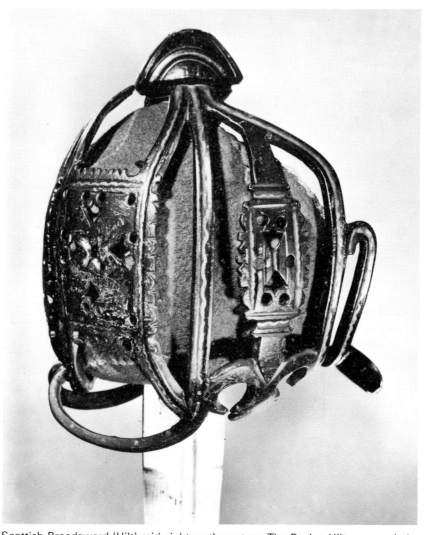

Scottish Broadsword (Hilt) mid eighteenth century. The Basket Hilt was made in Stirling. (Photograph by courtesy of Royal Scottish Museum, Edinburgh.)

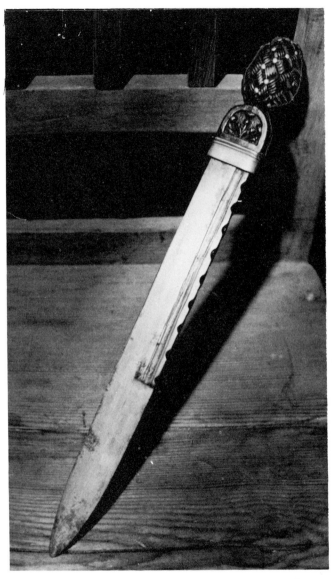

Scottish fighting dirk, mid eighteenth century or earlier.

progressed to the flintlock. Only one musket of distinctively Highland style has ever been recorded, but at the little town of Doune, near Stirling, and elsewhere, many beautiful pistols were made in the Highland style.

These pistols were fashioned completely of steel and were distinguished by the fact that they had no guards on the trigger, which was in the shape of a small ball. The Highland weapons were further distinguished by their butts, which either terminated in a heart shape, or curved inwards like a pair of ram's horns. They were fitted with a little detachable pricker between the 'horns' with which to clear the touchhole.

These beautiful and peculiarly Scottish weapons were usually made in pairs, and today no representative collection of firearms is considered complete without at least one example.

All of the weapons I have described are keenly sought after, both by collectors, and also by Scots overseas. As a result, a great deal of outright faking and 'cobbling up' goes on.

The few genuine claymores which exist are in museums or private collections, and it would be an event indeed if another genuine specimen were to turn up. Copies abound, however, and while most reproductions are coarse and heavy, this is not always the case.

Genuine hand and half and two-handed blades have survived in some numbers, particularly in the Middle East where they were highly prized, and specimens often turn up which can be dated right back to the Crusades. 'Claymores' have been made from these blades, and this gives the copies the advantage of lightness, for the true claymore was remarkably light for its size, weighing about seven pounds or so.

Highland pistols, particularly in pairs, fetch very big sums indeed when they come on the market. Well over £1500 for a good pair is common, but this is, of course, a field for the expert, and the expert moreover with a deep purse.

After the proscription laws of 1746, all broadswords had to be broken and surrendered. So while complete early specimens are fairly rare, many are offered for sale with old baskets 'married up' to later blades or even genuine old Continental blades.

Genuine broadswords are so much sought after—they usually fetch more than three figures—that the temptation to the unscrupulous is very strong. Really old targes or targets are almost never available, although Victorian and modern copies abound—but they are seldom good enough to deceive any but the most credulous.

Curiously enough, the genuine old fighting dirk is not nearly so prized as the tinselled Victorian specimen, and good ones can still be found. They cost £35 to £75, while the much inferior but showier Victorian examples fetch three times that amount.

97

My advice to anyone wanting to buy weapons or relics of the Scottish Highlands is to go to a dealer on whose knowledge and integrity he can rely.

21   Antique Pistols

When I earned my living 'On the Knock', or as that trade is described in Glasgow, as a 'Clapperton', it was my ambition to come on a matched pair of Scottish pistols. I never did manage to fulfil that particular dream, and perhaps it was just as well for my peace of mind, for I would not then have been able to pay the proper price for them.

I did, some time later, buy—from a convent of all places—a matched pair of double-barrelled pistols by Wogdon of London. This maker is recognized as one of the greatest of early-nineteenth-century English gunsmiths, and the specimens I came across were in mint condition, complete with case and spare flints, powder, balls and loading and cleaning equipment.

By this time I had an understanding bank manager and I was able to 'bid fair', which was fortunate for me, as the sister in charge of the finances had done some careful research into the present-day market for antique weapons.

Scottish pistols made in the Highland taste are very much sought after by collectors. I use here the word 'pistols' with care, for very few muskets or other type of long gun were ever made in the Highland style.

Indeed, only six years ago, at an English country house sale, an alert dealer bought for £10 a musket which was described as 'eastern' in the auctioneer's catalogue. The musket had been made in Dundee in the mid-eighteenth century. It was without wooden parts and in other respects followed the typical taste of Highland pistol-makers. The dealer put the gun back into auction, this time properly catalogued, and it sold at £14,000.

For the first 200 years after their invention, guns were fired by means of a smouldering cord or 'slow match' applied to the touch hole, which was simply a hole drilled at one end of the barrel. The poor general wanting to fight a battle could have all sorts of problems. At night, it was difficult to conceal the glow of the slow match, so surprise attacks were not possible and if it rained at all heavily, it was best to call things a day and go home.

It is not easy to explain to non-technically minded people (and that includes me) how a flint-lock works, but perhaps the best way is to recall how as a boy, to the despair of my mother who was trying to bring up five of us on a widow's pension of a pound a week, I would produce showers of sparks by striking my tackety boots along the cobblestones.

The first gun to employ this principle was called a wheel-lock because it utilized a little serrated wheel, just as we do today in a cigarette lighter, to strike a shower of sparks, not from a flint but from a soft mineral called iron pyrites.

A little later, towards the end of the sixteenth century, the true flint-lock came along, called in its early form the 'snaphaunce' lock. It is with these snaphaunce pistols, the earliest surviving from the seventeenth century, that we can observe the emergence of a distinctive Scottish style and a remarkable style it is.

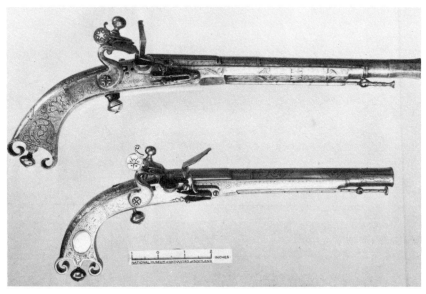

Typical all-steel pistols in Highland style (upper example by Alex. Cameron, lower by Alex. Campbell). Note the ram's-horn butts, ball triggers and absence of trigger guards. (Photograph by courtesy of the National Museum of Antiquities, Edinburgh.)

First of all, no wood was used in their construction. While a few were constructed partly of brass, the vast majority were made entirely in steel. Often the metal would be inlaid with silver, and when new would be blued against rust so that the overall effect was extremely beautiful.

There exists the record of an indictment in the burgh court of Edinburgh in 1560 where the prisoner is accused and 'Did ding sundry leiges on their heidis with his pistolles to their sair hurt and effusion of bluid'. Presumably the all-metal construction was helpful in the event of a misfire.

100

In any event, the all-metal butts terminated either in a heart or kidney shape or, typically, in the shape of a pair of ram's horns; the 'ram's-horn butt' in fact. Between the horns was a small knop which formed the head of a steel needle or pricker, which was used to clear the touch hole of powder foulings.

The actual locks were conventional in pattern, although a notable feature is a long belt hook attached to the backplate. Some of the earliest of these locks are Dutch importations and others follow the Dutch snaphaunce lines.

A sharp flint was screwed tightly into the metal jaws of the 'cock' and held secure by a leather patch. This cock sat on top of a long V-shaped spring which was compressed by pulling the cock back on its axis. When the trigger was pulled, the cock was thrown forward against a metal plate, the 'frizzen'.

In snaphaunce locks this metal plate was on a separate arm, but in the improved flint-lock it formed the cover of a 'pan' which held fine gunpowder. The flint struck the frizzen, jerking open the lid of the pan and sending a spark into the fine powder which in turn ignited the main charge in the barrel by means of the communicating touch hole. If the main charge failed to ignite, one had a 'flash in the pan'.

The triggers on Scottish pistols, however, were not of the conventional style. They were in the shape of a ball, a feature found elsewhere only on Circassian guns, and there was the complete absence of any trigger guard, usually considered necessary to prevent the accidental discharge of the weapon.

Gunsmiths existed in most Scottish towns, but with the exception of Edinburgh, where both styles were made, Lowland gunmakers worked to the patterns common to England and France. In the towns of the Highland marches pistols were made purely for sale in the Highlands. In one of them, the little town of Doune near Stirling, the pistol-making trade became so important and the workmanship so famous that even in the eighteenth century the Doune pistols were being copied in Birmingham.

I cannot today drive through the sleepy little town of Doune without seeing how it was 200 years ago. The great drovers of Highland cattle crossing the river beneath the castle and the row of pistol-makers' shops in the main street, crowded with drovers, hucksters and cattle dealers.

I know where I can find a pair of pistols by Murdoch of Doune. They have been in the same family for many years and they are still only a few miles from where they were made. It is some two years since I discovered these pistols and started to try to buy them. I have been promised them 'sometime, but no' jist the now', by the elderly owner.

101

Even a four-figure offer, my latest, has not been enough to produce a decision but I live in hope; both that I will eventually get my chance and that when it does come, I still have enough money to lay on the table.

22   Edged Weapons

Many years ago I bought from a pub in Perthshire a bundle of swords which in turn had been acquired by the publican, one by one, in exchange for a few pints.

Amongst this bundle, one sword remains in my memory—a basket-hilted broadsword complete in its scabbard. The 'basket' was fashioned from brass instead of the much more usual iron, and the scabbard, which was constructed in the ancient way of two slightly concave strips of wood, still had scraps of what had once been scarlet cloth remaining around the once splendidly gilded mounts.

It was the blade, however, which I found the most fascinating, for besides the usual legend of 'Andrea Ferrara' stamped in the centre, there was a Gaelic inscription damascened in gold just below the hilt.

Fortunately a friend of mine is (apart from being a great wag) a classical Irish scholar. I found my friend ensconced in his usual hostelry and handed him the sword. 'It says here,' he said, looking at the inscription, 'if you can read this you're too damn close.'

Once he had had his laugh, he gave me the correct translation—'I make sleep.' What a grimly poetic name for a sword! I only wish that I could buy it back now for many times the amount for which I sold it.

The collecting of weapons falls into two divisions: firearms and swords, or, more accurately, edged weapons, for thus are included all categories of weapons from pikes to bayonets.

Unless one has considerable capital, most firearms of quality are now well beyond the reach of the collector. This is not true, however, of edged weapons. They of course can be much earlier than the earliest firearms, and to anyone with a sense of history, they can be much more fascinating.

Most of the swords shipped out of Britain in the last few years have been of the showier Victorian variety; so the serious collector has suffered no great loss. Early and eighteenth-century examples are naturally rarer, although often costing no more than late Victorian tinsel. It is fairly accurate to say that any eighteenth-century sword costs roughly a tenth of a pistol of the same period and quality.

Very early (that is, medieval weapons) are more the province of the archaeologist, but eleventh and twelfth-century European blades which have been refashioned at the hilts in the Middle East, and which are genuine survivors from the Crusades, can still be found. These weapons often bear an early Frankish swordsmith's mark and when

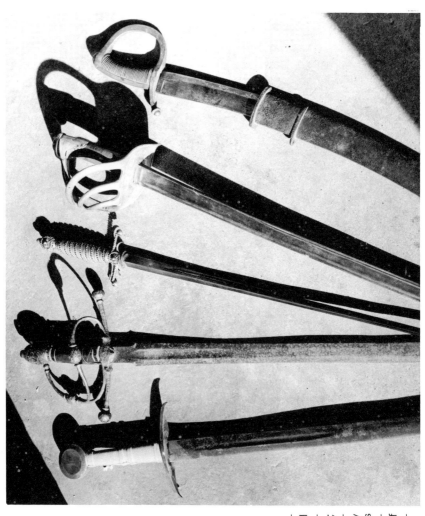

From left to right: Sixteenth-
century sword with pommel
restored; Early-seventeenth-cen-
tury sword with Frankish blade;
Gentleman's small sword common in seventeenth-century
Europe; British cavalryman's
sword of the late eighteenth century; Volunteer officer's sabre of
Napoleonic Wars, engraved 'Fife-
shire Local Militia'.

one considers their remarkable history and their cost at as little as £15, a specimen in my estimation would form an ideal basis for any collection.

European swords from this early period and indeed for several centuries afterwards are invariably long and broad-bladed, although very much lighter in weight than they look. They were designed to be swung rather than used to thrust, and often they needed the use of two hands to be wielded effectively. In an age when the upper classes went around the countryside like perambulating lobsters in mail and armour plate, the early sword had no 'basket' built on to its hilt, as the hand was normally protected by a glove of plate or of mail. Thus early swords can be easily distinguished.

As armour went out of use, the hand needed some protection. At the same time, sword play was becoming much more of a science than an exercise in armour bashing; so the 'basket' was developed to protect the hand and also to trap an adversary's sword point, while the blade itself became increasingly suited to thrusting instead of wild slashing.

Yet there are at least partial exceptions. Cavalry swords of the seventeenth century developed a single-sided blade, the 'backsword' as it became known; and in socially conservative areas like Scotland and particularly the Highlands, the beautiful but hopelessly impractical basket-hilted broadsword survived until its proscription after Culloden.

In the eighteenth century, the gentleman's small sword developed. This weapon was very beautiful and in the hands of a trained swordsman, utterly deadly. The blade became triangular in section in order to give strength to an otherwise frail slip of steel, and the hilt had only the protection of a simple 'knuckle bow' with, later, two 'shells' to guard the hand.

The finest specimens of this weapon were very expensive indeed— with hilts of silver, and gold inlay on the blue steel blades, but examples of simpler though excellent quality can be bought today for £25 to £50 or so.

The military and naval officers' swords of this period are heavier in pattern although they are most attractive, with gilt hilts and blades on which the blueing and gilding often survives. The scabbards were of leather with copper gilt mounts, the topmast of which often carries the name and address of some long vanished cutler.

During the Napoleonic Wars, many swords of diverse patterns appeared. This was a time of military innovation, although, sadly, on the British side at least, fashion rather than sound tactics determined the new styles.

The campaign in Egypt produced copies of the curved blades of Islam among the officer class of both British and French forces.

Those were the years of the fencible and yeomanry regiments raised

SIR RALPH ABERCROMBY. K.B.

51

Sir Ralph Abercromby, by John Kay of Edinburgh.

for auxiliary duties in Britain and Ireland and officered by 'part-time gentlemen'. Weird and gaudy were their accoutrements, and many of the Scottish officers have been immortalized by the gentle satire of the artist John Kay.

The cutlers and lorimers must have worked overtime turning out curved and decorated swords for those half-trained soldiers to belt to their gorgeous uniforms, judging by the number which still come to light, often extravagantly engraved with scrolls, cartouches, slogans and names of obscure military formations.

With all their fascinating history, edged weapons can be most satisfying to collect. Some indeed are rare and expensive, but most can be bought for £15 to £55, which makes all but the dearest very underpriced.

23   Collecting Glass

Glass is such an ubiquitous material, so much a part of our daily lives, that I am sure few of us take time to reflect on its origins and what, in fact, it consists of. This is a pity, for the story of glass is, to a large extent, the story of civilization itself.

Basically, glass is a substance known as silicate, whose commonest form is sand. To make silicate fuse together to form a mass capable of being shaped while plastic, two things are needed: the first is heat, and the second a fluxing agent, commonly either soda or potash.

It is not known precisely when glass was invented, but certainly it is as old as the most ancient civilizations and was familiar to the Egyptians about 3500 years ago, reaching them possibly from Babylon. A remarkable amount of this early glass has survived and it can be extremely beautiful.

However, while ancient glass is found in many colours and combinations of colours, it is never clear and colourless as we know it today, for the chemical knowledge essential to rid the material of its impurities was not available to the early glassmakers.

The technique of blowing glass was almost certainly an Arab invention, and can be dated to about 50 B.C. Before then glass vessels had to be made in moulds or sometimes the insides of bottles were formed by boring the glass, in much the same way as jade is still worked.

The art of glassmaking and glass-blowing soon spread throughout the Roman world, but for several centuries its artistic home remained in the Arab world. With the decline of Islam, however, the centre of world glassmaking moved to Venice and the lovely glass of Murano became renowned. This was soda glass, most attractive but too frail and brittle for deep cutting or engraving.

Glass of Lead

While glass was made in several countries, notably in Bohemia and in Holland and Germany, it was an Englishman who invented a new and remarkably improved type of glass, which was destined to give England and later Ireland dominating positions in the production of all types of high-quality glassware. The time was the last quarter of the seventeenth century, and the man's name was George Ravenscroft of London; his invention was lead glass.

Ravenscroft, a chemist, succeeded after long experiment in making a new type of glass, basically by adding lead to the traditional materials. This glass, much heavier and tougher than the traditional soda glass, had wonderful reflective qualities, particularly when it was cut into designs with facets, using the techniques of the lapidary.

Ravenscroft's lead glass is still made to the same formula today in most high-quality table glass produced in Britain. Often this type of

Left, typical English decanter c. 1790; left centre, early-eighteenth-century baluster stem glass; right centre, 'Silesian' stem sweetmeat glass c. 1720; right, Irish decanter, mould blown c. 1820.

glass is referred to as 'crystal', a term which can cause some confusion, for true crystal is a naturally-occuring mineral substance which owes nothing to the hand of man.

Genuine old drinking glasses can command very high prices indeed, and you are unlikely to come on one as a casual purchase. Stranger things have happened, however, and to illustrate what rare old glasses are actually like, I have included pictures of two among the small collection of glass illustrated here.

Both date from the early part of the eighteenth century and, although radically different in shape, their construction is typical of the period. As can be seen, the foot in each case is dome-shaped and,

109

apart from the pleasing proportions that this imparts, the shape has an important functional reason.

During the making of handmade glass, the white-hot metal is held (even today) on the end of a rod called a 'pontil', before the foot is attached. When the part forming the stem of the glass is broken off, a jagged and uneven end is left—the 'pontil mark'. If the foot of the glass were flat, this end would scratch any surface on which it sat, so the foot was made dome or conical shaped to eliminate this hazard.

These early glasses invariably show impurities in the metal and the scratches or striations typical of hand-working. Less easy to see, perhaps, but always present in glasses made before about 1830 is a small mark on the rim where the glassmaker sheared off the glass from his tool. This mark may be a slight bump or even a tiny section which is a trifle thicker. This was later eliminated by improved methods of working.

At various stages in history, glass in Britain has been taxed, but especially during the last thirty years of the eighteenth century when a crushing tax based on the weight of articles was imposed. As much of the glory of English glass was in its weight factor, due to its lead content, the tax dealt a severe blow to the English industry and to the few struggling Scottish glassworks.

Irish Glass

It's an ill wind, however, and as Ireland at this period had a measure of fiscal autonomy, the growth of glassmaking there within a few years was remarkable. Irish glass of this period will always be associated with beautiful decanters and heavily cut table ware such as jugs and fruit baskets. This lovely glass, which in some respects has never been surpassed, was also made in a variety of colours.

Perhaps the best known of this period is the pure deep blue obtained from cobalt and often referred to as 'Bristol blue', although it was made in various English and Irish glassworks. Often used as liners for silver and Sheffield-plated articles, it is remarkable how much of this Georgian glass you still come across, often separated from its original function and quite unrecognized for what it is.

Although, as I have said, it will mean either a lucky find or an expensive purchase to acquire a drinking glass of the early eighteenth century, such glassware as single salt and cruet bottles from the end of that century are by no means difficult to find, at prices ranging from a few pence to one or two pounds. Small items of Georgian glass with typical 'hobnail' cutting are still around and the edge of this cutting, by the way, will be nice and sharp—as distinct from the blunt feel of its later imitations in pressed glass.

Single glasses from the 1800s are not rare, and as these should seldom cost more than £10 or so, they are, I believe, well worth buying both as an investment and for the satisfaction they give, particularly if they are engraved or coloured, or both.

Good Georgian decanters cost quite a lot if they are early, but it is surprising just how reasonably priced decanters from the 1820s and 30s can be, especially if the neck is slightly chipped. These chips can often be reduced or even eliminated by careful grinding. A point to remember when buying glasses or decanters for use is that they look very different (and more attractive) when full!

Much Victorian table glass is rather graceless, but do not condemn everything Victorian because of this. The thing to appreciate is that a great deal of this glass is craftsman-made, and if it is pleasing in appearance and does not cost much, it is well worth buying.

24   The Rise and Fall of Scottish Pottery

The road that skirts the sea between Musselburgh and Prestonpans to the east of Edinburgh could hardly be described as romantic. The district has been made largely featureless by the detritus of old pit workings, with here and there the ruins of some colliery building amid the scrubby waste.

It is precisely this area, however, that in the eighteenth century was the very centre of the industrial heartland of Scotland: the small coastal strip beginning at Portobello and ending at Cockenzie. Not merely was coal won and shipped from here but salt, so very important in the days before refrigeration, was made in vast quantities in sea brine pans fired from local coal. Glass was also manufactured, the local kelp providing the necessary soda, as it did also for the considerable soapworks.

Another industry also flourished here, which in its heyday was of first rank importance in the economy of Scotland. This was the making of ceramics.

The manufacture of earthenware pottery is undoubtedly a very old craft indeed and in Scotland may well date back to Roman times and beyond. It is certain from records still in existence that pot works were well established in Portobello at the end of the seventeenth century, and by the first half of the following century they had spread, not merely along the shores of the Forth but west to Glasgow, where the large and important firm of Dinwoodie formed the nucleus of what was to become a major industry in the west.

The kind of pottery made by these early firms was initially brown stoneware, which was covered in a thin hard glaze formed by throwing handfuls of salt into the kiln when it was at maximum heat. Some of this stoneware was whitened by using calcined flints and white clay in the body, and about this time too the technique of making Delftware —earthenware glazed with an opaque, lead-based glaze—was imported from Holland.

In Glasgow, the delft made by Dinwoodie was well known and widely exported, particularly to North America. Many pieces of Glasgow Delftware survive and have been identified, and many more no doubt remain in homes and museums, classified as Dutch, for very little of this early Scottish ware bore makers' marks.

It is a curious fact that there is yet no Delftware which has been ascribed to any of the east coast pot works, although it surely must have been made in eastern Scotland, as it certainly was in the Newcastle area. The decoration of Delftware required a peculiar technique of fast and sure brushwork, as the unfired ware was highly absorbent and no corrections or alterations were possible.

A bowl which I own, and which is beautifully decorated in over-glaze colours, demonstrates the typical brushwork of the Delftware painter at its best. The bowl, however, which dates from about 1780, is made not in Delftware but in cream-coloured earthenware and is certainly from one of the east coast Scottish pot works.

Scottish pottery: Left, East Coast 'luggie' c. 1800; centre, Delft c. 1780 probably Glasgow; right, jug in 'Pratt' colours c. 1800. Gordon's pottery, Prestonpans.

This yellowish body and lightly-fired overglaze decoration is often ascribed to Portobello, but in my view it is typical of the work from the small potteries between Joppa and Musselburgh. The really significant thing about this bowl is that its decorator had learned his trade working with Delftware, and would have switched over to the new cream earthenware in the 1770s.

In Prestonpans itself no fewer than twelve pot works existed before 1800. Chief of these were the firms of Gordon and Watson. The story of the first works is to my mind both fascinating and sad. They made a very high quality ware and seem to have specialized in the type of jug known to English collectors today as 'Prattware'.

113

This ware was decorated in a variety of high temperature underglaze colours obtained from mineral oxides. This gave a palette of dull green, brown, orange and a brilliant blue which is at once distinctive and delightful. The themes of these jugs are typical: 'sailor's farewell' and the 'sailor's return', and commemorative portraits, particularly of that great Scot, Admiral Duncan. Other jugs, often oval in shape, have Jacobite themes and emblems.

The sad aspect is that by far the greatest part of this ware is classified as 'English-Staffordshire', both in the antique business and by others who ought to know better.

Gordon also made the little chimney ornaments or 'dabbities', so much a feature of Scottish working-class interiors. These were small and modelled 'in the round' and while they were often simple and even crude, the portraits of local working folk which most of them consist of have a directness, an honesty, and a compassion which makes them real works of art.

Gordon's rivals, Watson's, also made figures and jugs and mugs and it is fortunate for us that while few of their productions carry makers' marks, a great many carry inscriptions with names and even dates. Scots people seemed to delight in commemorating all sorts of events and anniversaries with articles of specially decorated pottery. By this means a jug carrying details of a ship's launching, or a bowl given to the incoming tenant of a farm or even a ploughman's wedding mug, can give us invaluable information as to period and provenance of other similar but uninscribed specimens.

Another and slightly later pot works in Prestonpans was Belfield's. This was started in the 1820s by the manager of Watson's pottery and a great deal of excellent work was produced there. Belfield's, indeed, were the only pottery destined to survive into the present century in Prestonpans, and the only firm in my opinion to achieve consistently high standards during the otherwise debased late nineteenth century.

Along the road to Musselburgh and past the busy harbour of Morrison's Haven, there once stood one of the most important of all the Scottish potteries. Here, as far back as 1755, it has definitely been established that a man called Littler founded a small factory making soft paste porcelain. A very few specimens have been identified, the 'key', as it were, being two mugs, specially commissioned and decorated with the Dalrymple coat-of-arms and the words 'Over Hailes'.

Once these mugs were thought to have been made at the early English factory of Bow. It was impossible, it was argued, that Scottish porcelain could reach this high quality at so early a date. Discovery of other unmarked specimens, however—none of which could possibly have come from Bow—and the existence of documentary evidence including that from the great Wedgwood, have quite definitely given Littler's factory and thus Scotland an important place in the history of porcelain.

Further potteries, mostly very small, lined the coast from Musselburgh to Portobello. At this village, just about where the Figgate burn entered the sea, stood two well-known potteries, one of which, Smith's, later to be known as Buchan's, survived on the same site until very recently.

Two mugs: the ship design is from Kirkcaldy (Robert Heron) c. 1840. The other, of the type generally attributed to Rathbone, Portobello, may be from one of the small potworks between Joppa and Musselburgh, c. 1810.

The adjoining property was operated by Scott Bros. in the 1780s and later, in about 1810, came under the control of Thomas Rathbone. Scott Bros. had the distinction of putting a maker's mark on quite a lot of their ware and one can still today come across their jugs in dark stoneware, coloured a pleasant chocolate shade with printed 'willow pattern' scenes in underglaze yellow.

Under the management of Rathbone, the pottery produced a great many plaques and figures in bright colours. These were of high quality and the figures tended to be rather larger and more mannered than those from Prestonpans. Commemorative ware, particularly marking the visit of George IV in 1822, was also popular and this at least is usually correctly ascribed today to Scotland, although there remains a habit of crediting Rathbone's factory with much of the production from neighbouring potteries.

115

Across the water, around the area of Kirkcaldy, and farther up the Forth at Alloa and Bo'ness, many other potworks operated for a great number of years. Perhaps the best known of these was the Gallatoun pottery at Kirkcaldy which about the year 1840 was acquired by Robert Heron whose son in the 1880s began production of the well-known 'Wemyss' ware, a brightly decorated range of earthenware which, although poorly potted, is much sought after by collectors today.

To describe the early pottery industry of Scotland with anything like comprehensiveness would require a volume of considerable size, for by the turn of the nineteenth century there were at least ninety potteries in operation, more than half of these in the West of Scotland and some making not merely earthenwares but also bone porcelain of a very high standard.

Unfortunately, the only work devoted to Scottish pottery is a book by J. Arnold Fleming originally published in 1923 and recently republished. While Fleming's book is undoubtedly valuable to the student both of Scottish industrial history and of ceramics, he concentrates on the second half of the Victorian era and displays a condescending attitude towards the productions of the early potters.

From about 1840 onwards, in common with British ceramics as a whole, the standards of Scottish potteries steadily declined, and perhaps the best work was produced by Belfield, and to a lesser extent by the Dunmore pottery in Stirlingshire. This period, however, is both artistically dull and fully documented, as most of the ware bears makers' marks.

There has existed in Scotland a peculiar apathy about this once-important aspect of her industrial past, and in comparison with the research done in such minor English areas as Newcastle, Scotland's record is a shoddy one. Unlike such major potters as Spode and Wedgwood, the small early factories did not publish pattern books of their wares. Identification of specimens, therefore, is a much more involved process. The very few early articles bearing makers' marks are invaluable for purposes of comparison, as are the more common inscribed pieces which can be checked against parish records.

The most important evidence, however, remains obtainable only by serious archaeological excavation on the sites of the old potworks which can provide supplies of shards and 'wasters', thus giving a complete and accurate picture. To my knowledge, and to our shame in Scotland, no research of this nature has yet been attempted, although it is now common practice in England and elsewhere.

The site of Buchan's works at Portobello has, I understand, now been acquired by Edinburgh Corporation, and some competent excavation may be undertaken there. As for the rest of the sites, they remain either as dilapidated buildings, or beneath colliery refuse. Work has begun by East Lothian County Council in a scheme to clean up the area of Morrison's Haven. It would appear, however, that the unique opportunity for an archaeological survey which this activity presents has been completely ignored.

25   A Tale of Three Finds

In the days of my youth I was discharged from the Army without any skills other than the destruction of my fellow men. Accordingly, I entered the ranks of that occupation which has become, in Britain at any rate, almost traditional to the Irish—navvying.

It might be thought that this activity is a far cry from the rather more sophisticated atmosphere of the antique salon, and indeed that is so. However, in the course of my excavating I discovered a great many things, mostly shards of pottery, and these I carefully took off my shovel and put aside for cleaning and further study.

The point is that a comfortable bank balance is not necessary for those with enthusiasm for antiques. Indeed, enthusiasm is the operative word, for it can lead to knowledge and also to love. Conversely, the possession of a great deal of money does not bestow with it the qualities I have mentioned, and I can think of a great many people who have stuffed their homes full of antiques, usually on a magpie basis, with the result that their collections range from the superb to the tawdry, and none of it can they either understand or enjoy.

The recirculation of items and Britain's richness in antiques will always ensure that the real enthusiast, even with little money, will be able to buy, discover and collect. Personally, I have the greatest fun out of making discoveries in this way, and to show what is still around I will discuss several items I have bought within the space of a few days.

It is largely to the civilizing influence of the Moslem peoples that we owe one of our greatest ceramic traditions: the tin-glazed earthenwares variously known as Faience, Majolica or Delftware. Europe first imported and then copied the many varieties of this ware made by Arabic-speaking peoples in the area ranging from Turkey to the coast of Spain.

The plate I bought is Persian and dates from the middle of the seventeenth century or earlier, and it is almost perfect. The colours are painted direct on to the opaque tin glaze, thus effectively covering the buff-red colour of the body.

The palette is typical of its place and period, being based on a deep shade of blue and a beautiful turquoise. A further thin glaze of lead covers the tin glaze. This second glaze, which is transparent, protects the painted surface and at the same time gives it a wonderful quality of iridescence.

I paid £10 for my plate and what a bargain it was. This I think is one of the bonuses of living in an area like Scotland. In London so many knowledgeable people are combing the shops that the chance of a bargain is much slimmer, while in Athens for instance such a piece would just about cover the air fare.

Pottery plate from Iran, seventeenth century.

An 'etui' is the name given to a small container, often of silver, which was used to carry such items as needles and scissors. Sometimes, however, etuis were made for a more specialized purpose, as in the example I bought for a modest £14.

I was attracted to this little silver container by its shape and style, which date it about 1750, and by the engraving of thistles, which makes it almost certainly Scottish. On the lid is engraved 'Dr Peacock', and on the side the inscription 'From a grateful Friend'.

Inside there are divisions for four small surgical scalpels, although

Scottish surgeon's etui c. 1750.

only three now remain, their steel blades still unrusted in their protective sheaths of tortoiseshell.

I was lucky to pay such a small sum for such a rare piece of silver, but even had I paid three times the amount, it would still have been a much better and more interesting buy than, for instance, a silver vinaigrette: such items to my mind being overpriced and over-collected.

While the English were perfecting their new lead glass and the Italians were losing their once dominant position in glassmaking because of the frailty of their beautiful soda glass, a new development was taking place in Bohemia.

Bohemian glass bowl c. 1830.

The Bohemians had for long been making a coarse but attractive glass with potash as a fluxing agent. This potash was in turn derived from wood ash, and so the glass was given the name of 'Forest Glass'.

In the seventeenth century, the Bohemians started to add limestone to their glass and eventually they perfected a type of heavy and yet quite soft metal ideal for wheel engraving. This glass, too, would take a coloured 'overlay' readily, and soon Bohemian glass became justly famous for decoration of this kind, an overlay of coloured glass on a core of clear glass with wheel engraving cutting off the colour to show the clear glass core.

The piece of typical Bohemian glass illustrated here—a bowl which although less than eight inches in diameter weighs more than 4lb—is rather a late specimen, dating from about 1830. About this time the

Bohemians developed all kinds of lovely colours as overlays, and this one, a pure sky blue, is most unusual and attractive.

Perhaps the shape has not the same purity of outline as earlier pieces, and certainly the rococo scrolls have lost their asymmetrical outline to conform with nineteenth-century taste, but at £10 it is a most beautiful specimen.

Although I am in the business of buying and selling antiques, and I now can and often do deal in rather expensive items, modest discoveries like these give me as much pleasure as ever.

Some of the early and genuine items you come across may be damaged, but in my view it would be a great mistake to scorn them on that account. Damage does not detract from the appeal of the article of real quality, while a later and perfect piece bought at a high price will not stand the test of time if the quality is indifferent.

26   The Story of Tin-Glazed Earthenware I

In the National Gallery of Scotland there is a small but very famous picture by Velasquez which depicts an old Spanish woman cooking eggs. She is holding in her hand a very typical dish of 'campesino' shape and I was immediately reminded of the painting when I recently bought just such a dish for a couple of pounds.

Various Glazes

The purpose of glazing pottery is, of course, to render it non-porous and to give it better wearing qualities. Traditionally glazes are of three sorts: lead glaze, salt glaze and tin glaze. Salt glaze was obtained by throwing handfuls of salt into the kiln at a critical temperature. A glittering and very hard glaze was thus obtained from the silica vapour released into the atmosphere.

Salt glaze, however, could only be used with stoneware—a kind of heavy earthenware with a proportion of crushed flints in the body and fired at a much higher temperature than ordinary pottery. The glaze was transparent but this quality, at a time when a white body was not available, was of doubtful value to the potter.

As a result, much ordinary earthenware was glazed with oxide of lead. This lead glaze was also transparent although much softer, and to cover up the unattractive body of the clay, mixtures of other metallic oxides were applied—copper to give green, or iron to give various shades of red.

These two kinds of pottery were made in Europe from early medieval times to the middle of the eighteenth century and later. However, from the great Arab civilizations spreading westward into the Mediterranean and east into Asia Minor came a wonderful new discovery—tin-glazed earthenware.

Tin-Glazed Earthenware

In essence, tin-glazed earthenware was made by adding a proportion of tin oxide to the lead glaze, thus rendering it opaque. The actual body used varied greatly, ranging from a sort of terracotta in Spain to a grey pumice-like colour in Anatolia. It was the glaze which mattered, however, for outside the Orient it was the first time a white ceramic surface had been available to the decorator.

For some time, for a period beginning about the ninth century, the island of Majorca acted as a sort of mercantile clearing house for the Moslem pottery exported from Spain and North Africa. When it was in due course imported into Italy, it became known as Majolica.

Later, when the Italians themselves started to make the new tin-glaze ware, it was referred to as Faience after the Italian town of Faenza, an early and important pottery centre. But it was by no means the only place where pottery-making was important: Deruta, Gubbio, Naples, Orvieto, Urbino and many others all play a part in the story of Majolica.

Velasquez: Old Woman Cooking Eggs. (Photograph by courtesy of the National Gallery of Scotland, Edinburgh.)

I was fortunate to buy some time ago, in a small shop in Fife, a lovely wine bottle made at Urbino in the last half of the sixteenth century. It had been used as the base of an electric table lamp and the shopkeeper was careful to point out that the price of £17 did not include the flex and fittings. I was not grumbling, however, for the twin of my bottle (unconverted, of course) is part of the Majolica collection of the Victoria and Albert Museum.

A wine flask from Urbino, made in the second half of the sixteenth century. It had been converted for use as a table lamp.

My wine bottle is simply painted in blue and this highlights one of the early problems facing the Majolica decorators. Only a narrow range of colours could be used on the opaque glaze, as these had to be able to withstand the high temperatures of the kiln when the glaze was fired to the body. The colours thus used were blue from cobalt and orange, red and green from mineral oxides.

The Arabs had a practice of applying a clear glaze over some of their wares such as tiles: this second glaze acted as a protection against wear and weather.

The Italians also used this second glazing technique, and they incorporated into the clear glaze a whole range of colours which were quite satisfactory if fired at lower temperatures. This technique, called 'coperta', together with the use of salts of gold to give a lustrous effect, brought the art of the Majolica potter to its full glory.

Barber's bowl, probably from Urbino, made in the second half of the sixteenth century.

'Glorious' is the only word to describe the decoration of Italian pottery during the full flowering of the Renaissance. The richness of the decorative themes, the allegorical and historical scenes, have given us something distinct and unique, which still delights; age in no way dims the original colours of Majolica, which remain as fresh as the day they emerged from the kiln.

Of course, do not expect to pick up Isnik or Hispano Moresque,

126

French Faience or Italian Majolica, for a pound or two. The very best specimens of any of this ware can rise to thousands of pounds but, and it is a big but, it is surprising what a keen eye and a few pounds can achieve.

Good early Iranian ware can be remarkably cheap and much more common than one might think. Not infrequently I come across really early Hispano Moresque or Isnik tiles, and French Faience of genuine age can be found—usually damaged, it is true, but cheap and charming for all that.

Reproductions abound, mostly carrying makers' marks, and since they form part of a vigorous tradition and are both attractive and cheap, they are well worth buying for what they are.

Occasionally, however, by a combination of luck and persistence, one can come across a really important piece lying unrecognized in some shop or saleroom. This, after all, is one of the joys still left to the collector in our part of the world.

Such a piece is shown here, a barber's bowl of the late-sixteenth century and probably made at Urbino. I came across this bowl in the West of Scotland just over a year ago. With its design of birds and berries, in colours of blue, ochre and green, it has, for the sum of £15, given me more joy I believe than anything I have ever bought, and nothing would induce me to sell it.

In the fifteenth century, Spain, much of Italy, and all of what we today think of as Holland were part of the Holy Roman Empire, and it was from Spain that the making of tin-glaze earthenware spread to Holland, to the town of Delft, and thence to the rest of northern Europe, including the British Isles.

Majolica has travelled a long way since its Moslem beginnings and we now move on to its later story in northern Europe.

27   The Story of Tin-Glazed Earthenware II

Before the Dutch town of Delft became a centre for the manufacture of tin-glaze earthenware, it was already a town famous for its brewing. It was natural, therefore, that the potters should often use a brewery sign as a mark, especially since the pot works were often housed in and sometimes owned by the breweries.

This Dutch tin-glaze ware is singular in that a great proportion of it carries makers' marks, and in northern Europe at least the term 'Delft' was soon in general use to describe all tin-glaze earthenware made outside the Latin countries and the areas of Moslem influence.

Of course, the traditional stone and lead-glaze earthenware had long been made in the Low Countries. It is this sort of pottery in the main that one sees so frequently depicted in paintings of Dutch peasant life by such artists as the Elder and Younger Breugels. It was not long, however, before the rather more expensive Delft ware came into common use in the houses of the new and prosperous burgher class in the towns.

The white or almost white surface of Delft was reminiscent of the fabulously expensive Chinese porcelain which the sailing masters had already started to bring back from their long voyages to the Orient; it naturally followed that much Delft was decorated in the Chinese manner.

So beautifully was this done that it is often very difficult, even for the expert, to determine if a piece is Dutch or Chinese merely by viewing in a specimen cabinet. It is only when these very high quality examples are handled, that by their 'softness', their light weight, and, of course, their lack of translucency, they are recognized as being Delft.

Although oriental styles of decorating remained common, the Dutch developed their own distinctly native touch which has the same homely appeal as much of their painting of the period. One sees this particularly on tiles, which are the most typical of all articles produced in delftware. These tiles were exported all over the world and there must in Scotland be thousands of seventeenth- and eighteenth-century fireplaces which are lined with Dutch tiles, the attractive and often narrative themes of the decoration having given delight to generations.

The surface of tin-glaze earthenware before it was fired in the kiln, and when it was ready for the decorator's brush, was highly porous. This meant that the decorator had to load his brush with just the right

This tin glaze plate from South Sweden or Denmark is from the second half of the seventeenth century; colours are orange, blue and green.

amount of pigment and work with swift and sure strokes on a medium where no erasures were possible.

To our eyes a great deal of the decoration on single-fired Delft looks astonishingly modern. Indeed, I cannot look at some of the later work of Picasso without being reminded of delft decoration at its most typical.

Like the Italians, the Dutch found themselves rather restricted by the limited colour range offered by the high-temperature pigments, so they used the 'coperta' technique which they called 'kwart'. This technique consisted of a 'cover' of clear glaze over the opaque lead glaze, which allowed low temperature colours to be used, a method of double firing usually reserved for more important pieces.

Typical mid-eighteenth-century Dutch Delft tiles.

In Britain Delftware was already being made by the middle of the seventeenth century and the famous blue and yellow 'dash' chargers, often depicting kings and generals, are typical of this period. Such places as Lambeth, Bristol and Liverpool all developed styles which can readily be recognized by the specialist. Little of this English ware is marked and still less is double fired, so that these factors, together with differences in the clay body, enable it to be classified correctly without confusion with Dutch ware.

Surprisingly, in view of the destruction of most Irish industry by the English maritime laws, Ireland produced some very fine Delftware in the eighteenth century. Places such as Cork, Limerick and Belfast were notable and in Dublin, Henry Delamain made pottery to very high standards.

The German and Scandinavian potters made Delft and, as might be expected, the south Germans tended to be influenced by French style,

130

East Coast Scottish bowl of the late eighteenth century. The bowl is of cream earthenware, but the delft style of decoration is clearly apparent.

while in the north their work was much more like the Flemish and Dutch. The Scandinavians, too, had their own tradition and much of their decorative work had a maritime theme.

I was fortunate enough, when in Sweden, to visit the Vaasa, that remarkable example of a seventeenth-century Swedish warship salvaged from the bottom of Stockholm harbour, where it had lain complete with its contents since it sank on its maiden voyage.

The plate I have illustrated here is from the same period and is Swedish or Danish. Similar examples were salvaged from the Vaasa, although I found mine in Scotland, and this brings me to the final and perhaps saddest part of my tale.

If I could, like Burns, 'Sing some song for puir auld Scotland's sake', it would in part, at least, tell the story of Delftmaking in Scotland.

The large works of Dinwoodie at Delftfield in Glasgow are well enough known simply because so many documents concerned with their export trade survive. Little serious work, however, has been done on the identification of specimens and the excavation of shards.

In the east of Scotland the same sad tale can be told. The bowl illustrated here comes from the area between Musselburgh and Portobello and was made about 1800, of creamware. But it has been decorated by someone who learned his trade as a Delftware decorator, as even the most casual comparison with the Scandinavian plate will show. It is, to me at any rate, quite obvious that Delftware must have been made in this area before its demise in competition with the new creamware.

In my view it is serious work of this nature—the study and comparison of unmarked specimens, the search for relevant documents and, above all, a detailed excavation of the old sites—which alone can provide a key to unlock the full history of Scottish ceramics. Surely the Scottish nation has sufficient scholars and resources to make some beginning to this kind of study.

Last year, the Irish organized an exhibition of their own Delftware which drew world-wide attention and went on later to New York. That Ireland, with a much more slender ceramic tradition than Scotland's, was able to do this makes me for one slightly ashamed.

28   Irish Silver

Back in the days when the pound had 240 pence, I took the notion of a working holiday in the Highlands. The idea was to do a bit of fishing and to see also what I could find 'on the knock'.

The fishing proved not too bad, but I was scarcely keeping my head above water with what I had managed to buy in the way of antiques, when I stopped for bed and breakfast, not very far from Inverness. My landlady served a delicious soup from an earthenware tureen with a nice old ladle which, as it poured, I could see was silver.

I complimented her on such a fine silver ladle, and she gave me a puzzled look. 'Oh it's only plate,' she said, 'all the cutlery I got at a house sale years ago is the same.'

Indeed it was all the same, but it was silver: Irish silver which, no doubt, with its curious markings, had resulted in its being sold as an odd lot of plate among kitchen furnishings and garden tools. The landlady and I struck a happy bargain for both of us, and not a little richer, I set off home.

Both silver and gold were worked in Ireland from early times and articles are still to be seen in the National Museum of Ireland in Dublin, which are of as fine workmanship as, and contemporary with, the artefacts of Attic Greece. The working of precious metals under the supervision of a guild certainly dates in Dublin from before 1498, although the original charter was accidentally burnt and, it would appear, not renewed until 1605 when a system of assay marks and makers' marks was instituted.

These marks have varied through the years, but until at least Republican times, Dublin silver always included a Harp Crowned, together with a date letter, plus of course the maker's mark.

In the year 1731 a new mark was added—the figure of Hibernia seated. This mark is the cause of much confusion in identifying Irish silver, for it is often mistaken for the figure of Britannia used on much early-eighteenth-century English silver to denote the higher or Britannia standard of the metal. Even in the trade, the Hibernia mark is often referred to as a duty mark because, coincidentally, Irish silver had to bear a duty of 6d per ounce (quite a large amount then) from the year 1730.

Ireland had of course a degree of independence until the Act of Union in 1801, and it was not until 1807 that the English duty mark instituted in 1783 as the Sovereign's head made its appearance.

Ireland at the end of the eighteenth century was a desperately poor country, but one is apt to forget that its population before the great famine was about the same as England's, a little over eight million. The prosperous classes were large enough to provide the economic base for flourishing guilds of silversmiths, not merely in Dublin but in most of the provincial towns as well. The marks on provincial Irish silver, like their Scottish counterparts, are many and complex, and examples are just as keenly sought after.

Distinctive marks are, however, by no means the most interesting aspect of Irish silver, for not merely is workmanship usually of a high standard, but often the design and even the function of the articles are uniquely Irish. The rococo style which originated in France and crossed to England about 1725, came late to Ireland, but the Irish craftsmen and designers took to it with singular enthusiasm and made from it a style both completely charming and very Irish.

Irish silver 'potato' rings, mid eighteenth century.

The basis of rococo is bold, asymmetrical scrolls which impart a lightness and exuberance often missing from its predecessor, the baroque.

The Irish rococo adds scenes from rural life, so that among the scrolls and leafy ornament we come across pigs and milkmaids, hens and cattle, church steeples, pheasants, and the poacher with his gun. It is a beguiling style, especially when it appears on such already attractive objects as cream jugs and those milk pails pierced to take a liner of Irish blue glass.

The most characteristic of all Irish silver articles, however, is the potato ring, although the term 'potato ring' is misleading as it was never intended to hold potatoes, cooked or otherwise, and indeed was not originally so called but by its correct name of 'dish ring', which shows its real function: a ring on which to stand a hot serving dish so that it did not mark the table.

It is a puzzle why these dish rings were made only in Ireland, for I cannot think of any which were not Irish. I have had at least one, not of silver but of Sheffield plate; that in itself is unusual, as it would appear that very little of this silver substitute was made in Ireland.

What one does come across are examples of 'duty dodgers', which are articles of silver either bearing no marks as they have never been submitted for assay, or false marks, or even genuine marks which have originally been struck on some small article of little weight and then cut off and 'sweated' on to a much larger and heavier piece.

The penalties for breaking the law in avoiding duty were rigorous and strictly enforced by the guilds, but these offences continued, more I suspect out of resentment against paying the duty than from a desire for gain, as the 'duty dodgers' are seldom inferior in the quality of silver used.

The dish rings illustrated here are two of a set of four made in Dublin in 1760. They show Irish craftsmanship at its most typical in the rococo style. The four would set you back about the sum necessary for a good saloon car, and come to think of it, would in the long term be a much better investment: I foresee no problem of obsolescence with Irish silver dish rings.

Postscript

Antiques are the articulation of the past. They are history, not expressed in words but in craftsmanship. They show the pattern of the way people once lived and the evolution of society, in vivid and exact and also evocative terms.

It is not for me to idealize the past. Poverty is never romantic to the poor, and in the past poverty was far too often the lot of too many.

The antiques that I handle daily in the course of my work do show, however, that the craftsman, at least, found a satisfaction and a dignity in his craft, however hard his life may have been. Today perhaps, we know a different kind of poverty from that of the past, a desolation of the human spirit.

Many of the antiques illustrated and discussed in this book were made by humble people to grace comparatively humble homes. They are, to me at least, all the more precious for that.

My calling makes me a fortunate and a privileged person. I still feel the same sense of excitement and discovery now that I first felt years ago when I went into the antiques business, lacking knowledge and money, but filled with a boundless enthusiasm.

It is my sincere hope that I have managed to convey something of this feeling in this book.